Bridging the Gap

Between College and Law School

Bridging the Gap

Between College and Law School

Strategies for Success

THIRD EDITION

Ruta K. Stropus & Charlotte D. Taylor

CAROLINA ACADEMIC PRESS

Durham, North Carolina

Library of Congress Cataloging-in-Publication Data

Stropus, Ruta K.
  Bridging the gap between college and law school : strategies for success / Ruta K. Stropus & Charlotte D. Taylor. -- Third Edition.
      pages cm
  Includes bibliographical references and index.
  ISBN 978-1-61163-224-8 (alk. paper)
  1. Law--Study and teaching--United States. 2. Law students--United States--Handbooks, manuals, etc. I. Taylor, Charlotte D. II. Title.

  KF283.S77 2014
  340.071'173--dc23

                        2013044620

Carolina Academic Press
700 Kent Street
Durham, North Carolina 27701
Telephone (919) 489-7486
Fax (919) 493-5668
www.cap-press.com

Printed in the United States of America

This book is dedicated to our fathers.
You loved us and taught us and brought us together to teach others.

Contents

Acknowledgments

This book would not be possible without the help, love, and dedication of many wonderful people, including Cathaleen A. Roach, who served as a role model and a mentor to both of us.

We would also like to thank the following people who made this book possible:

Our colleagues:

Stephanie Juliano
Andrea Kaufman
Kenneth A. Rosenblum
Susan Thrower

Thanks for your many suggestions and comments and for reading our draft and returning it on such short notice.

Dan Ursini

For inspiring us to keep our dream of publishing this book alive.

Our research assistants:

You have helped us in more ways than we can recall and kept us working, even when we did not want to.

Francis Cermak, DePaul University College of Law Class of 2000
James Derry, DePaul University College of Law Class of 2001
Tracy Hamm, DePaul University College of Law Class of 2000
Mike Isroff, DePaul University College of Law Class of 2001
Moira Murphy, DePaul University College of Law Class of 2008
Robert Sabetto, DePaul University College of Law Class of 2002
Shannon Verner, DePaul University College of Law Class of 1999

We would also like to express our thanks to the former Dean of DePaul University College of Law, Teree E. Foster, for her support of the Academic Support Program and of our research for this book.

About the Authors

Ruta Stropus is the Director of Attorney Recruitment and Professional Development at the Illinois Attorney General's Office and a former Assistant Dean and Professor. She previously served as director of the Academic Support Programs at both DePaul University College of Law and at Northern Illinois University College of Law. She received both her undergraduate degree (summa cum laude, 1986) and her law degree (1989) from Loyola University of Chicago. After graduating law school, she practiced in litigation with McDermott, Will and Emery, and Sachnoff & Weaver, Ltd, two prestigious law firms in Chicago. She has previously published a law review article addressing concerns about the current trends in legal education titled *Mend It, Bend It, and Extend It: The Fate of Traditional Law School Methodology in the 21st Century.* 27 Loy. L.J. 449 (1996).

Charlotte Taylor is the Assistant Dean for Student Services at the Touro College Jacob D. Fuchsberg Law Center. She previously served as the Assistant Director of the Academic Support Program and then as the Assistant Dean for Multicultural Affairs and Student Support Services at DePaul University College of Law. She received her undergraduate degree (1992) from Bradley University in Peoria, Illinois, and her law degree (1996) from DePaul University College of Law. After graduating law school, she practiced insurance defense with the law firm of Greene & Letts in Chicago.

Preface

Travel Advisory

Quite a bit has changed since we embarked on the journey of writing this travel guide, of sorts, for law school. Most significantly, the legal market has turned upside down, leaving many new graduates without promising economic prospects. Indeed, going to law school is no longer a guarantee of financial security; rather, saddled with six figures of debt, many students question whether they should have taken the journey at all.

Therefore, we add this preface to the third edition. Like all travelers, you need to ask some pretty basic questions before setting off on a journey.

> Do I really want to go here?
>
> Do I think this will be a trip of a lifetime? How will it change my life? What are my expectations?
>
> It is a very expensive journey. How will I pay for it? What will a large educational debt mean to my other goals, such as homeownership and family?
>
> Even if I expect to do very well in law school and land a high-paying job, what if those expectations aren't met? What if that doesn't happen?
>
> Have I spoken to others who have taken this journey lately? What were their impressions? Would they do it again?

One of my former students recently remarked: "I went to law school thinking I would be Abraham Lincoln; instead, I'm doing document review." Despite media depictions, the practice of law is not glamorous. The work is often tedious, the hours long and the costs to service law school loans immense. The very practice of law is changing, as clients are moving away from billable hour arrangements and demanding that attorneys provide a more competitive price for their services. In some environments, the supply of attorneys exceeds demand, thus substantially driving up competition.

So, let us caution you before you begin. Seek advice. Listen to contrary opinions. Crunch the numbers. Question your motives. Set realistic expectations. Above all, make sure you know the answer to this question: "Why are you going to law school?"

Introduction

Have you ever embarked upon a long journey? You probably began thinking about your journey by looking through some travel books. There are generally two types. The first is the general guide—how to travel on a penny a day, how to backpack through Europe, or great dining in the Middle East. The second is country-specific—Kenya, China or Japan. Obviously, there are benefits and drawbacks to each type of guide. The ones that are broader in scope give you a nice overview, perhaps some history and tips, but do not provide enough specific information. The specific guides, on the other hand, although ripe with details, do not provide vital context—where does this country fit in with others in the region? What are some general customs and tips that apply when travelling? Wouldn't it be nice to have a guide that could combine both the general and the specific?

The travel analogy extends to law school in this and many other ways. For example, just like there are many self-guided travel books, there are many "self-help" books written for law students and would-be law students. Generally they too fall into two categories: those that offer general advice and those that are tailored to specific topics of study (i.e., a contracts study aid, a torts study aid, etc.) Until now, no book has integrated the two and offered even more. This book offers you an explanation of legal pedagogy, a helpful approach to the law school experience, a process of study, class participation, exam taking techniques and much more. Most importantly, because we teach these skills using these materials, we know that they actually work! We have tried out these tips and techniques on hundreds of law students, and revised and modified them based on student feedback; therefore, unlike any other "self-help" texts, this one is based on the experiences of actual students like you.

How Does *Bridging The Gap* Integrate the General and the Specific?

Bridging the Gap integrates the strengths of both the general and the specific advice texts and offers you more. We cover all of the following areas:

We explain the "why" of law—we provide you with the context you need to understand why law school is taught in a certain manner, why you read cases as primary texts, and why law school professors test in the way they do. This context will provide you with the necessary insight you need to better understand the law school experience.

We explain the "how" of the law—not only will we provide context, but we will also provide process. We will take you through a step-by-step process that will help you adapt to the law school setting, and we do so in a way that draws upon and connects to your past learning experiences. Rather than tell you that what you have learned and how you learned it in the past is irrelevant, we will help you build upon and draw on your strengths.

We explain the "what" of the law—in addition to context and process, we offer specific hypotheticals that will help you practice this process. We will take you through actual law school hypotheticals in the first year subjects so that you have many opportunities to practice the process. This is an interactive text. Instead of merely reading, you will participate in the learning process. By interacting with the text, you will take the context and process and make it your own.

Because *Bridging the Gap* combines the best of both worlds (general advice and specific subject study aids) and provides you with the information you need, you can expect better results than if you were using specific study aids or general advice books individually. Specific study aids are not effective. Although they do provide you with a summary of basic law principles, they do not provide context or process. They do not

Characteristics	General study aids	Specific subject study aids	*Bridging the Gap*
Provides summary of law in certain area		✓	
Provides practice problems		may offer one or two	✓
Provides general information about law school	✓		✓
Provides a process for how to respond to law school exams			✓
Provides information on reading cases, briefing, and outlining	✓		✓
Provides general exam taking tips	✓		✓
Provides a link between past experiences and law school			✓
Links the "what," "why," and "how" of the law			✓
Offers advice on time management	some		✓
Offers advice on troubleshooting —what to do when things go wrong			✓

teach you how to write a good examination answer. General study aids, on the other hand, may provide some context, but they do not emphasize the process and do not give you an opportunity to practice that process. We strongly believe that, in comparison to these two types of texts, ours will yield more favorable results, especially in light of our experience of teaching hundreds of law students how to succeed both in the classroom and on the exam.

What Can I Gain from Using This Book?

Unfortunately, no classes address law school environment or expectations. In fact, very few, if any, of your professors will address what the law school examination will look like and how you should approach it; therefore, you could write an answer to a law school question and think you did well, when, in actuality, you offered a poor response. Unless you know why it is that law school does what it does, what you should focus on, and how to write a good law school examination, your responses will not be adequate. Instead, they will look something like the following:

> Whether Bob can sue Sam for negligence depends on whether the court follows the *Smith*, *Jones* or *Rodriguez* cases on subject. In *Smith*, the court found defendant liable because she owed a duty to plaintiff. However, in *Jones*, the court did not find the defendant liable because although *Jones* owed the plaintiff a duty, he did not breach that duty. Finally, in *Rodriguez*, the court agreed with the *Smith* case and found the defendant liable when it said that *Rodriguez* owed plaintiff a duty of care. Here, the court is likely to agree with the *Smith* and *Rodriguez* courts and find that Sam owed Bob a duty and is therefore negligent.

Looking at this response, you might think that it's just what the professor is looking for—it answers the question and quotes several key cases. Without a guide or mentor to take you through and explain: (1) what the professor is looking for, (2) why this response is not the best for purposes of the examination, and (3) how to write a "good" response, you might never get the grade you expect. Without help, you might never know how to write an answer, which, like the one that follows, will earn top marks:

> Whether Bob can sue Sam depends on whether (1) Sam owed Bob a duty; (2) Sam breached that duty; (3) Sam's breach of duty caused Bob's injury; and (4) Bob's damages resulted from the injury. First as to duty, Sam would argue that Bob owed him a duty because of their relationship as guardian and ward. In *Jones*, the court held that an adult that is entrusted with the care of a minor owes that minor a duty of reasonable care. As in *Jones*, where a minor was left to the care of an adult, Bob, a minor, was entrusted to Sam's care for the day. Sam accepted that duty by telling Bob's mother, "Don't worry, I'll keep an eye on him." The second issue of breach is more complicated....

We want to bridge the gap between your expectations and law school reality; between your previous learning and the law school experience; between understanding the process and applying it to actual problems; between the answer featured previously and the one you will write after reading this book. To make the most of this book, however, you must interact with it. Do all the problems and compare your answers to those provided. We hope to demystify the law school experience, explain many useful techniques for not only surviving but also thriving in law school and provide exercises so that you can practice the techniques. We hope to accomplish these goals by using the travel metaphor as our guide. Because law school is, in so many ways, like traveling to a strange and foreign land, we believe this metaphor is especially apt. You are embarking on the most strange and consuming—but fascinating and rewarding—trip of your life, and we hope to give you some tips and insights along the way.

Bridging the Gap

Between College and Law School

Chapter 1

The Law School Experience

Law school is a strange and foreign place, much like a strange and foreign country. The language and the customs are unfamiliar, yet one expects a successful trip. We hope you will use this chapter much as you use a travel guide or brochure to prepare for your journey. Before heading out, make sure you investigate your destination.[1]

The History

Law schools use what is commonly known as the Socratic method for teaching, especially in first year courses. Some argue that this method is harsh and ineffective. Others maintain it fosters some basic lawyering skills.

To fully appreciate law school culture, all "travelers" should know something about law school history. Its development is quite interesting. Originally, lawyers didn't even go to school; law students trained to become lawyers by "reading the law."[2] Those wanting to learn the law apprenticed themselves to a practicing lawyer, who introduced and taught the law to them.[3] Students certainly learned practical skills through the apprenticeship method, which provided "hands on" experience from the beginning. Unfortunately, they often lacked knowledge about the law itself.[4] The hole in this method was obvious: imagine, for example, knowing how to fill out forms for a sales contract but not knowing a thing about what makes a contract valid and enforceable.

Given its weaknesses, out went the apprenticeship method. In its place came the lecture method of teaching.[5] The lecture method should be familiar, as it still dominates most undergraduate institutions.[6] Students gathered in a classroom, listened to a professor lecture about "the law" and memorized the rules.[7] Using the lecture method, material is often presented from the general to the specific. For example, in a business class, the professor may begin his or her lecture by saying: "Today class, we will talk about contracts. Specifically, we will discuss binding contracts and non-binding contracts. But first, what is a contract?" In this situation, students learn some basic, general information about contracts and then move on to specific information about binding and non-binding contracts. On the exam, the student will be asked to repeat this information (both the general and the specific) to the professor. The lecture method gave students the opportunity to learn substance; for example, they knew something about contract law. The disadvantage was that students didn't learn to **practice** law. The hole in this method is even more obvious: imagine knowing all the legal rules regarding contracts, but not having any idea about how to draft a contract.

Enter our appropriately named trailblazer, Christopher Columbus Langdell. Perhaps affected by the "scientific" age in which he lived, Langdell believed that law could be taught the same way as science, through the scientific method.[8] In other words, Langdell reasoned that if students read actual cases instead of text books and then discussed those cases in a question-answer exchange with an instructor, they would not only learn the law but would also learn problem solving skills.[9] Using the same example, in a law school Contracts class, the professor might start a class by discussing a case in which the court did not find a legal contract to be enforceable because the parties were minors. The discussion may then move on to another case in which the court did not find a legal contract enforceable because the subject matter involved an illegal act, a contract to sell drugs. In discussing both cases, the professor will ask students to point out the specifics of each case: the parties, the facts, how the case came to court, and the end result. In this situation, it is the student's task to put the cases into perspective with the rest of the class materials. The student must take the specific information he or she has gotten from class (the facts of each case) and deduce the general idea that the professor is trying to teach.

Langdell believed the purpose of law school was to train legal "scientists": to help them discover, by reading cases, a pattern of reasoning and then adopt and apply that pattern or reasoning to solve similar problems.[10] Thus, this method would teach students both law and process. Langdell, who served as Dean of Harvard Law School,[11] implemented his method with great success. His method caught on elsewhere, and the rest, as they say, is history. The "Langdellian" method has since taken firm root in law schools from coast to coast and has been the method of teaching American law for over a hundred years.[12]

This history is important because it provides a cultural context. As a traveler, one certainly feels more comfortable in a country once he or she knows not only the customs but also the historical reasons why the locals are acting the way they are. The same applies to the law school experience. Students who realize the method behind the law school madness tend to adapt more readily to this new environment. Remember that the Langdellian method is meant to help develop analytical skills. As one commentator put it, "The method not only causes the student to think; it makes him think twice."[13]

The Customs

Law school is a formal and hierarchical environment. Do not expect the warmth of a small town.

Many law students are shocked at the formal and hierarchical environment in law school. Some have come from campuses where students and professors are on a first-name basis. As one student put it, "I come from a place where I used to discuss a topic with Mary (her Prof.) over beer after class." With few exceptions, those days are gone. Law school professors usually address their students by last name, and they expect to be called Professor so-and-so at all times. In class, the professor will call on you to answer her questions without giving you much time to reflect upon your response. Law school professors and administrators are not mean; instead, they are following a tradition that mandates distance between teacher and student.[14]

Whether the law school classroom experience differs radically from your past experience depends on the size of your college. For example, first year law students normally attend classes in groups of about 100. Those coming from a small liberal arts college where a "large" class consists of twenty students may find a law school class quite shocking. On the other hand, those coming from a state university, where "large" sometimes means up to 400 students, may find the size of a law school class shocking for quite different reasons. Obviously, individual attention is hard to get in a class of 100; unless you are "on" (meaning that you and the professor are involved in case discussion), you may find yourself buried in the crowd. Try not to space out. Stay engaged.

Prepare yourself for the trauma of being called on in class. Unlike undergraduate classrooms, where student participation is usually voluntary, in law school you most likely will not know when you will be asked to speak. Some students suffer extreme anxiety and depression because of the often harsh in-class questioning.[15] Try not to perceive the persistent questioning as a personal attack; it's not. Keep in mind that even the most tenacious professor is not trying to humiliate you; rather, her goal is to refine your analysis of the issue at hand. If you find the questioning too much, volunteer for questions that you feel confident answering or try to envision questions that the professor might ask while reading a particular case before class. Remember that this method is supposed to engage, challenge, foster independent thought, and develop analytical skills.

Many have criticized this formal, hierarchical law school environment.[16] Criticism is certainly justifiable: who wants to travel to a place where people have a reputation for being taciturn and aloof? Although some law students thrive despite this less-than-warm environment, many students find the environment stifling. Indeed, some recent scholars have noted that the argumentative, confrontational, controlling, impersonal, logical, and abstract[17] culture of law school interferes with student learning. Others have called the method used to teach law students "infantilizing, demeaning, dehumanizing, sadistic, a tactic for promoting hostility and competition among students, self-serving, and destructive of positive ideological values."[18]

Perhaps the method currently in use is flawed; perhaps someday it will be different. For now, however, law schools show no sign of changing, so no alternative exists other than coping with the culture as is. To take our travel analogy a step further, why avoid a trip to a fantastic country simply because the people who live there have a reputation for being rude, especially to those who don't speak the local language? Instead, be prepared in law school to encounter some less-than-friendly locals.

Do not take on attitudes that protect your ego at a cost of long-term success. For example, try not to "tune out" and settle for just getting through the experience.[19] Never become antagonistic toward the professor or other classmates; this is not a time to protect your ego by "mobiliz[ing] defensive aggression."[20] Neither of these extreme coping mechanisms will benefit the short-term goal of student learning or the long-term goal of effective lawyering.[21] Instead, develop positive coping mechanisms. For example, after a particularly stressful day of non-stop questioning by a professor, get a group together and treat the "victim" to lunch to celebrate surviving the "legal hazing." This type of gesture not only helps soothe the ego, but builds a sense of community as well. Remember, the process is a new way of learning, so by definition it will be difficult to adapt. Memorizing material and regurgitating it at a later date might be easier on the spirit, but it does not foster the type of problem solving skills that all great lawyers possess and use on a daily basis. No one is interested in hiring an attorney who knows all the rules by heart; instead, one wants an attorney who knows how to use those rules to win the case. Establish a group of fellow travelers to get you through the initial adjustment.

When you hit some rough spots, find people in the community who are dedicated to making your journey easier. Seek out the Academic Support office or the Dean of Students; either can offer assistance. Remember, your tuition dollars are funding this trip; if you find something or someone interfering with your journey, let them or someone else know. Many student organizations also offer invaluable guidance for the traveler who is temporarily disoriented or disenchanted and needs to get back on track. Your school wants to ensure that your journey is worthwhile, so take advantage of all it offers. Remain upbeat during the journey. Indeed, the ability to stay positive during law school will help you get through the rough spots and may be the difference between simply surviving and actually thriving in law school.[22]

Packing for Your Trip

Before getting into the specific skills and strategies necessary to succeed in law school, it is important to take an inventory of the skills you already have and understand why those skills brought you success in college or in your career. Think of this assessment as deciding what to pack for an upcoming trip. Before buying new clothes for a trip to the Bahamas, you first look in your closet to see if any of the clothes you have will suffice. If you have only sweaters and jeans, chances are you'll be uncomfortable in the Bahamas. Maybe you have tee shirts and shorts, but they aren't appropriate for the beach. Maybe you'll be dining formally, and tee shirts and shorts won't do. If you find that you need new clothes, you must figure out what to buy and how your new purchases will work with what is already in your closet.

We suggest first examining the skills you used in college or in your career before we discuss acquiring new skills for your journey through law school. Consider how you prepared for class and for exams in college. Did you read and highlight passages from the textbook? Did you take notes on the text and class discussions? Did you memorize highlighted material from a textbook or memorize your (or someone else's) class notes? At work, did you learn how to do your job "by doing," gaining insight with each project or task you completed? Alternatively, did you learn by reading a manual of "how to" information, to which you could refer whenever you needed? Did you use someone else's work as a model, tweaking it and making adjustments until it suited you and you knew what you were doing?

If you used any of these methods, your study skills were probably very useful to you in college and in your career, and you no doubt achieved a measure of success. You will need to use the same skills in law school, but you will need to build on them and acquire new skills because law school material is taught and tested differently. In college, a lot of material is taught using the lecture method, requiring you to memorize information gleaned from a textbook or in the professor's lecture. In law school, material is taught using the Langdellian or Socratic method (as previously discussed) and is tested using the problem-solving method. Because of this difference in teaching and testing, students entering law school need to acquire quite a few new skills for studying and preparing for exams if they are to succeed.

On a typical law school exam, the student will be given a fact situation and will be asked whether or not her client will win in court. See the sample question below.

Sample Law School Exam Question

Thirteen-year-old Bobby, the school bully, beat up on Steven and Jamal, also thirteen, every day. Unable to take it anymore, Steven and Jamal went to the school cafeteria to talk to Steven's older brother, Kevin, about how to stop Bobby. Steven reminded Kevin that he still owed them a favor for helping him with his science project a month ago. Kevin, eighteen, agreed to "take care" of Bobby for Steven and Jamal, but only if they gave Kevin their allowance for the next six months. Both Steven and Jamal agreed. Just to be sure, Jamal snatched a napkin to record the agreement and all three signed it at the bottom.

The next day at school, Steven and Jamal were called into the principal's office and informed that Bobby was in the hospital with a broken nose and a broken arm. Afraid of the consequences, Steven and Jamal refused to pay Kevin his "fee." Kevin cannot afford a lawyer on his allowance. He has come to you and wants to know if he can get his "fee" from Steven and Jamal.

Obviously, this is unlike any case the student has read; reading and memorizing the facts of cases from the book will not get her anywhere. The student cannot repeat the facts of any of the cases she read about contracts to adequately answer the question. Here, the student must engage in problem solving. The student must determine the specific problem (often called the "issue"), identify the rule of law that applies, and apply that law to the new facts to determine who will win the lawsuit. The student must "own" the information and be able to employ it to reach a solution.

Because of the drastic differences in how material is taught and tested on exams, you will need to acquire new skills to complete your journey through law school.

What to Bring

A mind trained in analytical thinking and an ability and desire to write are staples for the journey through law school.

You may or may not have had a pre-law advisor who guided you to some of the courses that might help you prepare for law school. Regardless of your major, if you are still in college and have the opportunity to select electives, make sure that you take logic (usually offered by the philosophy department) and writing courses. If you have been out of school for a while, enroll in a refresher course, such as a graduate or continuing education course or two. The number of students who somehow fail to realize that the practice of law involves a great deal of writing is astounding. If you hate the thought of spending the bulk of your time composing anything from a partnership agreement to a court memo, law school probably is not for you. Although popular culture portrays lawyers as spending their days in courtrooms in front of juries and nights in fancy restaurants impressing clients, most of the work of lawyers, especially new ones and certainly law students, is far less glamorous. Law school demands many hours outside the classroom just reading cases (expect three hours out of class for each hour in class, or about fifteen hours per class each week), and countless more completing legal writing assignments (give yourself at least ten to fifteen hours for a five-page paper); in practice, these numbers go even higher. Nothing will help you succeed more than the ability to read and retain large amounts of information and write about it effectively. Start developing these skills now.

Consider taking courses that require reading difficult texts and synthesizing large amounts of complex material into a workable format; upper level literature and philosophy courses are excellent choices for acquiring these skills. One of the problems students face at the outset of law school is reading the required text. The bulk of what you have read up to now likely has been what we call "descriptive texts." In college, you probably read textbooks on various subjects. In your life or career, you probably read manuals and guides on how to accomplish particular tasks, operate equipment, assemble toys, and perform various other functions. Otherwise, you undoubtedly read novels, articles, and other informational pieces, for different reasons. What these texts all have in common is that they each explain a topic or skill; in short, they are all descriptive. In terms of quantity, you were probably expected to read several pages a night from your college textbook. At work, you were probably expected to get through reading material at your own pace to fully understand it. In law school, both the quality and quantity of reading is radically different. In terms of quality, you are not reading descriptive texts or books; instead, you are reading original cases, often very old ones written in outdated, difficult-to-understand language. You cannot zip through and skim the pages to get a feel for the topic. You need to spend time, and lots of it, just to understand the case. And, just when the quality changes, so does the quantity. Instead of reading several pages a night, you are very likely to be assigned a hundred pages a night. Many students simply are not ready to read so many pages of this dense text. There are online options that can help develop these skills. Such sites include www.4lawschool.com or others. They cannot substitute the actual experience of reading and processing the cases, but can help you learn to analyze the main points of the case. In many cases, the decision is lost in seemingly complicated legal jargon, and these sites can help you break down the information.

Prepare by reading. Anything. Now. Train yourself to read a large amount of pages per night. Become a reader; to truly maximize this experience, become a reader of difficult material. Don't read cases in your spare time. Instead, if you are still in college as an undergraduate or a graduate program student, enroll in courses that require you to read difficult material while forcing you to analyze, rather than just describe. For example, a senior seminar that requires students to describe readings in a paper is not as beneficial as a seminar that requires students to read several works and then synthesize and analyze them. If you are out of college, practice on your own. Find a few works on an abstract topic that interests you, such as philosophy or religion. Read and analyze the material, focusing on the key elements of each idea. How can each concept be summarized? What elements do the concepts share? How do they differ? Although it may not sound like a fun way to spend your time, it will get you into the practice of analyzing and synthesizing ideas. For those students who have been in the workplace before law school, you have the advantage in that you engage in problem solving of some sort in the workplace. However, law school problem solving, unlike workplace problem solving, is based on theory. Given this context, students who have been out of school for some time might want to take a continuing education course that focuses on applying theoretical concepts. However, avoid speedreading courses; law school demands that you read **slower**, more deliberately and reflectively, not faster.

Reading, unfortunately, is not enough. To truly succeed in law school, you must also be a writer. Many observers have lamented the decline in writing in colleges and universities,[23] and critics have pointed out that fewer graduates each year are capable of writing at an adequate level. Far too many students react to writing courses with fear and revulsion. For law students particularly, such a response is unfortunate simply because the legal profession offers no way around writing. Even the student receptive to writing papers, however, must understand that writing in law school, or "legal writing," is very different from writing a paper for college or even for a graduate program. Legal writing is technical writing.

Like your reading experience, the writing you've done in the past was probably descriptive rather than analytical. Research papers, essays, even letters you wrote probably described rather than analyzed and synthesized. Even when you were asked to analyze someone else's work, you most likely described it. In law school, you will be asked to analyze a problem through writing. You will be expected to take apart the problem, look at each part of the problem individually, and come up with a solution. Some find this process stifling because of the emphasis on structure. Even if you do love to write, be open to the experience of learning a certain style of technical writing very different from what you may be used to.

Some students encounter a different problem: they have little writing experience or none at all. Here is another way undergraduate experience differs from law school. Unlike college, there is no way to avoid writing in law school, or in law practice for that matter. Lawyers communicate; it's their vocation. Communication takes one of two forms, written or oral. Contrary to the popular media's portrayal, most lawyerly communication is written. In fact, the most common question law firms ask potential associates is, "Can you write?" That's it. Not, "Can you argue in front of a judge?" or "How comfortable are you speaking in front of a group?" Instead, the focus is on written communication skills.

One of the most important courses in law school is legal writing, because it introduces students to analysis and synthesis; in short, it forces students to "think like a lawyer" while allowing them to see the thought process on paper. Give the course the attention it deserves. While you probably won't knock out a paper in one all-night coffee-and-Snickers binge, you will, through struggle and rewrites, begin to understand how lawyers communicate with each other, their clients, and the courts. There is no way out of this one. If you still have the chance before law school, conquer your fear of writing by taking a course or two that demands solving problems on paper. Although it might be harrowing now, it will ease some of the pain and anxiety of writing later on.

If you have been out of practice with reading and writing, or if your undergraduate program did not emphasize these areas, enroll in a course or two at a local university or community college. Seek courses that require reading, digesting, and applying information to solve problems. Certainly, difficult courses cause short-term pain, but they will provide critical long-term experience. Perfect your writing ability by practicing it. If you have not had an opportunity to learn grammar and composition skills, do so now; grammar and punctuation are not taught in law school, but they are essential to a lawyer's craft. Remember, words and language are the lawyer's fundamental tools. Lawyers are professional mouthpieces; the ability to manipulate and use language is often the distinguishing feature between an excellent attorney and a poor one.[24]

This is not to say that if you are a math major, a chemist, or a scientist who is starting law school in a month, you are already behind. Indeed, many "hard science" majors have wonderful analytic and problem solving abilities. While some English majors struggle with the abstract reasoning aspect of law, the science majors struggle with the verbal representation of the analysis, not the analysis itself. Whatever your past experience, know that you will bring both strengths and weaknesses to your legal studies. If you are prepared to build on your strengths and overcome your weaknesses, you will succeed in this new realm.

Preparing for Rough Terrain

Competition, held as one of the hallmarks of a good legal education, is perhaps overemphasized in law school. As you will soon discover, special privileges await those who make it to the "top ten percent" of the class after the first year. Additionally, special privileges await those who reach the top ten percent *and* make law review, write an article, serve on an editorial board, or participate in moot court. Unfortunately, those looking for a high-paying, big-firm "Grisham" job must be practical super-heroes for a shot at the "big-time." Can it be done? Sure. Do you need to be the smartest in the class? No way. Can anyone make it? No. By definition, only ten percent of the class ends up in the top ten percent. Some students will expend every ounce of energy they have to get to the top; many of them will never get there because they don't take the best approach.

Healthy competition is good; it keeps students on their toes and drives them to improve and succeed. But what pervades some law schools is more than a little healthy competition. Some students attempt to attain their goals with a cutthroat, "dog-eat-dog" approach. They hide books the class needs for assignments. They spread rumors about potential areas the professor will test. They proclaim that all responses given in class that day were completely irrelevant. These folks hinder constructive, cooperative learning by fostering paranoia and fear. Refuse to buy into their insecurities.

To maintain your center, remember that a successful lawyer is one who engages in collaborative problem solving, rather than competitive undermining of colleagues. You cannot do well in this environment if you rely only on your own memorization skills and prior academic successes. In law school, cramming and a mild interest in the subject will not win the A it once did. Indeed, it might not even earn a C. Understandably, many students find the dearth of shortcuts in law school a very difficult adjustment. In fact, some students admit that they "didn't work all that hard in college" and still managed to pull top grades. Even if you were able to cram in college, law school requires constant commitment and daily effort.

Most importantly, keep a healthy perspective. Law is not and need not be mystifying. With the skills we will outline in the following chapters you can learn, work hard, play and even sleep, all while conquering law school.

Getting Around

Law school is very much like exploring a foreign country without a map. Expect to get lost. Expect to be frustrated and confused. Expect, at times, to be frightened. Remember, however, that most "travelers" make it out alive and feel good about having found their own way.

The Langdellian method was not as foreign to law students when it first took hold. Indeed, most law students at the time had been exposed to this type of questioning in college. Moreover, "[s]tudents in Langdell's classroom had an undergraduate liberal education in rhetoric, logic, philosophy, science, and mathematics that served as a foundation for the case method."[25] They were accustomed to professors' unending questions and students' responses in an attempt to "discover" the truth. Indeed, Landgell's method was similar to the one used by Socrates, who questioned his students, on the theory that they would both discover "truth" together.[26] (Think of it as the Detective Columbo way of learning: listen, take notes, look perplexed, ask questions. Find the murderer). However, students preferred the lecture method because it made life easier: answering questions and applying facts to solve problems demands much more than taking notes and memorizing information. In fact, "[i]nitial reaction to the introduction of the [Langdellian] method was negative, extreme, and immediate."[27]

Given the rough road ahead, how do you navigate? How do you find your way through all the cases? First of all, remember why you are reading cases. You are learning not only the law but also legal analysis. You are being taught to "think like a lawyer."[28] Remember solving for x? Faced with an algebra or chemistry equation, your mission was to solve the problem by finding the missing piece. And so you did: x = 5 or 2 or 0; never did x = 5 or 2 *or both*. Never did the equation change to suit the circumstance. One answer always existed; you just had to find it. Unlike other disciplines, law rarely provides "one answer." Rather, in law, the best we can do is provide "an argument." More often than not, each argument has a solid counter-argument. In addition, in law, the "equation" may change; that is, the approach or even the rule of law can change or evolve to suit different circumstances. The equation is not fixed.

This can be one of the most maddening aspects of law school. Unfortunately, "when a student is set to expect a 'right' answer, it does not occur to him that there may be several 'right' answers, and that, given this state-of-affairs, it isn't the answer which is so important anyway but rather the questions to which the answers are related."[29] Put another way, don't expect to learn any "right" or "wrong" answers in law school. Although there may be stronger or weaker arguments, there is very rarely a "right" or "wrong" answer.

This drives students, especially first year students, bonkers. How can supposed "solutions" be so ambiguous? Why does every question provoke another question in return? Why would a professor "hide the ball"? Often, the more a student is comfortable with ambiguity, the less stress she will experience in law school.[30] Learn to love the grey. Rather than emphasizing right and wrong, professors assess the strength of students' arguments. Another math analogy illustrates this principle: rather than solve for x, show your "proof." What steps took you to your conclusion? Treat law more like geometry than algebra: the ultimate conclusion can vary as long as the proof logically leads to it.

Too many students think law school is about learning the rules; if that were true, students would memorize statute books and legal treatises, which they don't. Instead, you are learning how to solve legal problems. Recall the adage: give a man a fish, he eats for a day; teach a man to fish, he eats for a lifetime. The same principle applies: you are learning how to fish. Be patient. Expect to get lost. Expect to be frustrated. Expect to learn in a new way. Expect to examine material critically, explore logical implications, and discover faulty reasoning. If you can adapt to the legal environment and construct individualized ways in which to process a tremendous amount of information[31] (and we hope to show you some of those ways in this text), then you will enjoy this journey.

Avoiding Tourist Traps

Most law schools only test students at the end of the semester or at the end of the year. Don't misconstrue having only one final exam as an excuse for not studying throughout the semester.

Most college courses offer students ample opportunity for performance evaluation and feedback: quizzes, midterms, papers, presentations, and finals. At any given point in a course, a student can gauge her performance and progress. Such feedback is not only a sound educational practice, but a sound psychological one as well; the ego can adjust to small disappointments (blowing a quiz) and temper it with improvement (acing a test). Unfortunately, most law school courses do not evaluate students frequently, nor do most law professors provide the level of feedback students may be accustomed to. Indeed, most law classes evaluate students only once a semester, and only at the very end of the course. While this might seem like nirvana to some, it is extremely unfair because it does not prepare students adequately for the exam.

Imagine learning to play tennis by reading about tennis, watching tennis matches, and discussing tennis mechanics, but never actually playing a set until the final day of class.[32] Think of how nerve-wracking it would be to have an entire grade riding on one match for which you've never actually practiced. Yet most law schools operate this way: an entire semester of case discussion with no opportunity to test problem solving skills until the very end. Do not misconstrue having only one final exam as an excuse for not studying the entire semester. Unless you practice the skills, you will not do well on the exam. Learning to "think like a lawyer" takes time; you only begin to learn how to identify issues, articulate rules, apply them to facts, and draw conclusions when you see these steps in action over and over again in a variety of contexts. This doesn't mean you shouldn't practice with small hypotheticals, but be aware that final examinations will require sorting through complex fact patterns, spotting numerous issues, articulating different rules, and devising several arguments. You should test yourself using small hypotheticals throughout the semester with or without a study group. Later, you should try to tackle some comprehensive exams and get feedback on your answer from the professor or an Academic Support Professional.

Traveler's Advisory

Work hard, but work smart. The Langdellian method is far from perfect, but it can be conquered.

Remember that Langdell devised his new approach to teaching law in response to the shortcomings of both the apprenticeship and lecture methods of training legal professionals. Unlike your predecessors, you may never have been exposed to this type of teaching before. Certainly, if you were a science major, you have used the scientific method to prove a hypothesis. If you were a math major, you have resolved problems before by solving for "x." If you were a liberal arts major, you have certainly read and discussed original, difficult texts to reach a conclusion; however, you probably have not engaged in the type of classroom discussion in which one professor drills one student in front of a hundred or so of her peers, on the cases assigned, and on many variations of the cases. You may not have experienced the dreaded questioning, "Well, Ms. Smith, what if the light had not been red but yellow? What if the defendant didn't see the light because the sun was in her eyes? Would that affect the outcome of the case? How? Why?"

Now that you're prepared for the journey and are aware of some of the details, let's explore some of the skills you need to succeed. The following chapters introduce, describe, and illustrate each of the skills that will allow you to maximize your talents and hopefully minimize your stress.

Endnotes

1. Much of the information contained in this chapter is derived from an article on law school methodology. Ruta K. Stropus, *Mend It, Bend It and Extend It: The Fate of Traditional Law School Methodology In the 21st Century*, 27 Loy. U. Chi. L.J. 449 (1996).

2. Arthur Austin, *Is the Casebook Method Obsolete?* 6 Wm. & Mary L. Rev. 157, 158 (1965).

3. *See* Kurt M. Saunders & Linda Levine, *Learning to Think Like a Lawyer*, 29 U.S.F.L. Rev. 121, 127 (1994).

4. *See* Austin, *supra* note 2, at 160 (noting that "the apprenticeship method failed because it was tightly geared to the pragmatic mechanics of the law").

5. Reconstruction, urbanization, the dawn of the Industrial Revolution, and a new emphasis on science and technology together ushered in an era of professional public service after the Civil War, and colleges developed programs to meet the demand in various disciplines. Law was no exception.

Although a few law schools had been established (one as early as 1779), it wasn't until approximately 1870 when the concept of a legal education truly materialized. Paul Carrington, *Hail! Langdell*, 20 L. & Soc. Inquiry 691, 695–704 (1995). *See also* Albert J. Harno, *Legal Education in the United States*, 52 (1953) (noting that by 1870, "changes in legal education were in order" to resolve new complexities in law requiring knowledge and skill beyond black-letter learning).

6. *See* Saunders & Levine, *supra* note 3 at 127–28.

7. *See* Austin, *supra* note 2 at 160.

8. *See* Carrington, *supra* note 5 at 708.

9. *See* Harno, *supra* note 5 at 54.

10. *See* Austin, *supra* note 2 at 162.

11. Langdell served as Dean from 1870 to 1895. *See* Carrington, *supra* note 5 at 691 n.1.

12. Despite a history of opposition that still pervades today, Langdell's "technique endures as the mainstay of legal education." Alan A. Stone, *Legal Education on the Couch*, 85 Harv. L. Rev. 392, 406 (1971). Interestingly, after centuries of employing this methodology, Harvard is now considering taking a different track. Jonathan D. Galter, *Harvard Law Decides to Steep Students in the 21st-Century Issues*, N.Y. Times, October 7, 2006, at A10.

13. Steven A. Childress, *The Baby and the Bathwater: Salvaging A Positive Socratic Method*, 7 Okla. City U. L. Rev. 333, 349 (1982).

14. Not all commentators agree that meanness is all that bad. Indeed, one commentator has noted that "[t]eachers unwilling to cause such pain ... are not as helpful as they might be to students preparing themselves to deal with human conflict." Carrington, *supra* note 5 at 748.

15. Phyllis W. Beck & David Burns, *Anxiety and Depression in Law Students: Cognitive Intervention*, 30 J. Legal Educ. 270, 286 (1979).

16. For a sampling of articles criticizing the methodology, *See* Duncan Kennedy, *How the Law School Fails: A Polemic*, 1 Yale Rev. L. & Soc. Action 71 (1970); Karl N. Llewellyn, *The Current Crisis in Legal Education*, 1 J. Legal Educ. 211 (1948); Andrew S. Watson, *The Quest for Professional Competence: Psychological Aspects of Legal Education*, 37 U. Cin. L. Rev. 93 (1968).

17. *See* Lani Guinier *et al.*, *Becoming Gentlemen: Women's Experiences At One Ivy League Law School*, 143 U. Pa. L. Rev. 1, 93 at 62 (1994).

18. Stone, *supra* note 12 at 407.

19. Michael E. Carney, *The Narcissistic Concerns in the Educational Experience of Law Students*, 18 J. Psychiatry & L. 9, 20–21 (1990).

20. *Id.*

21. B.A. Glesner, *Fear and Loathing in the Law Schools*, 23 Conn. L. Rev. 627, 635–40 (1991).

22. *See* Michael J. Patton, *The Student, The Situation, and Performance During the First Year of Law School*, 21 J. Legal Educ. 10, 31 (1968). Patton notes that students who are unable to delay gratification and need to see immediate and tangible results tend to be more negative about the law school experience than those who are able to delay gratification and have a positive outlook on the educational experience.

23. Ernest L. Boyer, *College, The Undergraduate Experience in America*, 73–79 (1987).

24. *See* Stropus, *supra* note 1 at 471 (noting that modern law firms expect new associates to digest court decisions, apply sound analysis, and "communicate ... both orally and in writing in a comprehensive and intelligent fashion.").

25. Saunders & Levine, *supra* note 3 at 183.

26. *See* John O. Cole, *The Socratic Method in Legal Education: Moral Discourse and Accommodation*, 35 Mercer L. Rev. 867, 869 (1984). Actually, the Langdellian method is more similar to the Protagorean method than the Socratic way of teaching. Whereas Socrates' goal was for the student to gain self-knowledge, Langdell, like Socrates' rival Protagoras, sought to teach students "how to develop equally plausible arguments both for and against a given proposition." Richard Neumann, Jr., *Perspec-*

tives on Legal Education: A Preliminary Inquiry Into the Art of Critique, 40 Hastings L.J. 725, 729 (1989).

27. Paul F. Teich, *Research on American Law Teaching: Is There a Case Against the Case System?*, 36 J. Legal. Educ. 167, 169 (1986).

28. Debate abounds as to what it means to "think like a lawyer." For purposes of our discussion, it is the ability to "think precisely, to analyze coldly." Karl N. Llewellyn, *The Bramble Bush* 116 (1930). For a deeper explanation about how students are taught to think like lawyers, *see* Saunders & Levine, *supra* note 3.

29. Michael J. Patton, *The Student, the Situation, and Performance During the First Year of Law School*, 21 J. Legal. Educ. 10, 69 (1968).

30. B.A. Glesner, *Fear and Loathing in the Law Schools*, 23 Conn. L. Rev. at 634.

31. *See* Patton, *supra* note 18 at 21–27.

32. Cathaleen A. Roach, *A River Runs Through it: Tapping into the Informational Stream to Move Students from Isolation to Autonomy*, 36 Ariz. L. Rev. 667, 673 (1994).

Chapter 2

What Is Your Learning Style? Travel Style?

Similar to how you prefer to travel, you should make sure you know your preferred learning style so you can determine which study tips and techniques presented here will work best for you.

I have several friends who all travel to work differently. One friend loves excitement and adrenaline, so he prefers to bike along the lakefront (in Chicago) to travel to work. Another friend enjoys taking the commuter train so she can read the paper, check emails, and relax while not worrying about driving. Unlike both of them, I prefer to drive (usually fast, I have a reverse commute with little traffic), so I can listen to the radio and sing along.

Long distance travel is also different for different people. Some people prefer to drive so they can stop along the way to eat or stay overnight. By driving, these people control how quickly or how leisurely they will reach their destination. Others like to fly to get there quickly, whereas some prefer to travel on the train so they can sit and enjoy the ride.

The same way you plan your travel, you should plan your studying and determine what is going to work best for you. I want you to think back to college or even high school. What was your best class? When did you get that A or A+? What did you do to get that grade? Did you write a paper? Take a test? Did you study alone or with a group? Did you re-read the book and your notes? Or, did you make flashcards or a chart or graph the concepts? Knowing your preferred learning style will help you adapt and use the best study techniques to learn more efficiently and more effectively. This will not only allow you to work hard, but also work smart.

What Are the Different Learning Styles?

Many experts, including those who have studied education at the elementary, high school, college and graduate levels will tell you that there are many different learning styles. They will also say that most people exhibit a combination of multiple learning styles. This book defines and explains the three major learning styles, but there are many different learning styles that can be explored through additional research!

Visual

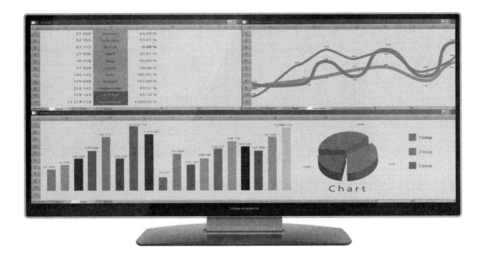

Visual learners are those who need to "see the picture" to understand it.[1] They like professors who use PowerPoint presentations with pictures and graphs and charts. I am sure you have heard the phrase, "A picture is worth a thousand words."[2] This phrase is true for visual learners. A picture, chart, or graph of the concepts and how the concepts fit together will help the visual learner absorb the material so he or she can retain it. We recommend that visual learners make flowcharts (see the chapter on Putting It Together, Part Three: Flowcharting), and also consider making their own PowerPoint Presentations to explain the material to their study group, or for recall and memorization. Visual learners can make a picture to represent each element of battery or burglary and use that to help them memorize the elements of the crime for the exam.

Auditory

Auditory learners need to "hear" the information to absorb it.[3] Giving auditory learners tons of information to read in a book is not helpful. They do well with a professor who lectures or who gives regular review sessions. If the professor lectures and tells stories, this helps the auditory learner remember the material. This student might be quiet in a study group, but would do well. For auditory learners, we recommend getting books on tape (CDs or MP3s), and/or making their own audio recorded lectures to listen to during their commute, or to reinforce the material. When thinking about the information, if the auditory learner can "hear a story" to attach to each case or concept, "the story" or "the association between the story and the concept" will help him or her learn the information.

Kinesthetic

In the words of NIKE©, kinesthetic learners need to "JUST DO IT."[4] These people are your friends or family members (for me, my brother) who put together the bookcase without the instructions (and use all the parts and it won't fall down). Kinesthetic learners enjoy physical activity when learning. These students are those who like to organize and lead the study group. They like to make flash cards and re-organize the course materials. Many kinesthetic learners will take a bit from the other styles by making a flowchart or recording their own lectures, and once it is done, they have learned and absorbed the information. These are the students who will make an outline and keep redoing it, and by the time they are done, they no longer need the outline because they understand the information to the point that it is memorized.

What Is Your Learning Style?

By now, some of you reading this chapter will already know your learning style. You were able to identify with the definitions and descriptions and know how you should be studying and what techniques will work best for you. For those of you that are still unsure (and are probably a combination of a couple of learning styles), you should consider a learning style assessment. There are several online assessments. Some are available at no charge. One that we recommend is the VARK Questionnaire available online at www.vark-learn.com. VARK provides a guide to four learning styles: Visual, Aural (Auditory), Read-Write, and Kinesthetic. They have a wonderful free online questionnaire that takes less than eight minutes to complete. Once complete, VARK provides you with results that list your scores in each area (visual, aural, read/write and kinesthetic). You can see which area has the highest score. In addition, the results include your learning preference, and you can click on additional links on their website for study strategies that apply to your learning preferences. There is an optional personalized learning profile report that you can purchase as well.

Before we knew about the VARK Questionnaire, we gave our law students the following Personal Exam Evaluation.

Exam Evaluation—Personal

The purpose of this questionnaire is to help YOU determine how and why you did not do as well as you should have on your exams. Therefore, it will be to your benefit to answer the questions as honestly and accurately as possible. Please complete this questionnaire and give it to me at least 24 hours before our individual conference.

Name_____ Section_____

Please list the following:

Class   Professor   Type of Exam (Essay, Short answer, MC)

_____

_____

_____

_____

1. How would you evaluate how prepared you were for exams? Please explain. 10—very prepared, 1—not prepared at all.

2. Please circle the following law school/exam taking preparation methods that you used and tell me how much study time was spent on each one.

<u>Method</u>   How many hours per day? Hours per week?

Reading (re-reading cases)

Reviewing with a study group

Listening to lectures on tape

Flowcharting

Outlining

Making flash cards

Memorizing Rules

Practice Exams on your own

Practice exams with your study group
Other (please specify:_____)

3. In which of your substantive courses did you perform the best? Why do you think you performed better in this subject than others?

4. In which subject did you perform the worst? Why do you think that was so?

5. Did you study ...

    Alone in a quiet environment?

    Alone in a noisy environment? (Like a coffee shop)

    With others by explaining things with your study group?

    With others by listening to your study group?

    By making flash cards or flowcharts?

    By reading from outlines or study aids?

    By listening to lectures on tape?

    By looking at flowcharts or diagrams?

    By getting the big picture first?

6. Which method worked best for you? Why?

7. Knowing what you now know about law school exams, if you could re-do last semester, what would you do differently?

What would you do the same?

8. Thinking back on the entire exam period, was there anything that happened the day of the exam, the day before the exam or during the exam that impacted your performance?

With slight modification, this evaluation can be completed by any high school, college, or law student to help determine how to learn best and how to study. This evaluation is NOT meant to give a specific learning style, but rather to encourage students to engage in self-reflection and self-efficacy. We would require our students to complete the evaluation and then discuss their answers to help them determine what study strategies worked best for them.

Only you can really determine what works best for you and what you need to do to learn and process the information so that you can retain it for later. The same way you don't need someone to tell you how travel to work or to your vacation destination, we hope you will use the information presented in this chapter to decide how you will learn and study best.

Endnotes

1. M. H. Sam Jacobson, A Primer on Learning Styles: Reaching Every Student, 25 Seattle U. L. Rev. 139, 150 (2001).

2. A picture is worth a thousand words has been attributed to Frederick R. Barnard, who published an ad in Printer's Ink in December 1921 with the phrase: "One Look is Worth a Thousand Words." Barnard later published another ad in March 1927 with the phrase "One Picture is Worth Ten Thousand Words" and it was labeled as a Chinese proverb that would later be attributed to Confucius.

3. *Supra* note 1 at 151.

4. JUST DO IT is a trademark of the shoe company, NIKE, and one of their most famous ad campaign slogans, which was coined in 1988. Jeremy W. Peters, *The Birth of 'Just Do It' and Other Magic Words*, N.Y. Times, August 20, 2009 at B3 (New York Edition).

Chapter 3

Learning to Read and Brief Law School Cases

After reading the introduction and the first chapter, you are now ready to begin. In law school, along with "learning to think like a lawyer," you are also expected to "learn the law" and learn how to apply it to a factual situation. In order to learn the law, you must first extract the law or rules from cases. You accomplish this by reading and briefing each case. You are probably thinking, "I already know how to read, so what's the point of this chapter?" The point is that the material you will read in law school, mainly court opinions edited and collected in casebooks, is very different from the material you read in college; therefore, in order to read, absorb, and understand cases, you must adopt a different approach. First, let us explore how and why law school reading material is different.

Reading in College

In college, most of your reading assignments, excluding literature, consisted of descriptive text. This type of text is used in college to suit the purpose of college learning, which is to provide greater understanding of a subject. In order to explain the subject, the author typically defines a concept or topic. Then general information is provided about that topic, before moving on to more specific information. For example, in business contracts, first the author might state what a contract is. Next, she presents general information about contracts. This could include such information such as the history of the first contract and the evolution of contracts; that is, she presents background information to explain the concept and use of a contract to expound on the definition. Last, she presents specific information about contracts, such as how and why they are formed and the different types of contracts (e.g., employment contracts, contracts for the sale of goods, etc.).

College texts that are descriptive are usually easy to understand because they are straightforward; the author defines a concept and then moves from general information to more specific information. While there are exceptions, reading for class tends to be uncomplicated. On the other hand, the books you will use in law school, primarily collections of edited appellate court decisions called "casebooks," are rarely descriptive, straightforward, or uncomplicated.

Reading in Law School

In law school, most of your reading assignments will come from a casebook. Although most casebooks consist of written decisions, or "opinions," from appellate courts,[1] they also contain brief introductory materials and notes related to the cases. Casebooks are used in law school to teach students to think like lawyers and to teach the law. Unlike college, in which texts aim to provide a greater understanding of one subject, in law school, casebooks are assigned to teach the law (i.e., rules) and, at the same time, the process of problem solving (i.e., the application of the rules) to a new factual situation.

In order to achieve this dual purpose, when reading each case, you must (1) extract the law or rule from the case and (2) apply the rule to different factual situations. These two tasks can be rather difficult, depending on how the opinion is written. More often than not, judges do not write cases saying, "The law in this case is…" or "The real problem here is … and in order to solve it we must decide…." If they did, reading and understanding cases would be easy because the format would be consistent and the logical steps leading to the conclusion would be clear. Unfortunately, it isn't that simple. In law school, you must engage in problem solving from the beginning (in reading even your very first case) to determine what is important about each case. Before we discuss specific tips and techniques for reading cases, we will define and describe the concept of case rules.

All law is made up of rules, and all rules can be broken down into smaller pieces or parts, called elements or factors.[2] Most cases explain, define, describe, broaden, or narrow rules. What are rules? What are elements or factors? Very simply, a rule is a statement of the law that proscribes what a person can do. For example, you may read a case in which the court was asked to decide if a dog owner violated the city's leash law when she had her dog on a leash but routinely dropped it and allowed the dog to chase a ball on a vacant lot. Ownership of the lot is in dispute. In deciding this particular problem, the court quotes the city's leash law, which states, "All dogs must be on a leash when in public." This is the rule.

Before you can analyze whether this particular owner violated the leash law, you must isolate each element of the rule and consider it separately. The elements are the specific conditions of a situation to which the rule applies, like a checklist of requirements. Here, the three elements are dog, leash, and "in public." If we have (1) a dog, and the dog is (2) in a public area (whatever that means), then we must make sure that the dog is in fact (3) on a leash to comply with the law. Students are quick to jump to the conclusion: "Of course the owner violated the law," before they assess each and every element of the rule. Before you answer any question "yes" or "no," always ask yourself, "Does this problem fit the rule?" "Has each and every element of the rule been satisfied?" In our dog example, although we do indeed have a dog, it is unclear whether the dog was in a public area (the ownership of the lot is in dispute) or whether the dog was leashed (what does the statute mean by "on a leash" — that the dog have a leash or that the leash be held by a human being?) The conclusion that "of course the owner violated the law" is hasty because it is unclear whether each and every element of the rule was satisfied.

Things You Need to Know before Reading Your First Case

Obviously, travel is a bit easier if you know what to expect. Likewise, reading a case is easier if you know what to expect. Usually, in the rush "to just get to it," law school professors do not explain how to read a case; they just expect students to know how it's done. Reading a case, however, is not like reading a textbook, a periodical or any other text. You need to have the necessary background before you can truly "read" a case. Here's what you need to know. Please note that although we have given you "the basics"—the information has much more depth and breadth than we've provided here.

The Dual Court System

"St. or fed."

The United States has a dual court system. The metaphor we will use to explain this duality is that of a small business with two departments, accounting and marketing. Think of the United States as a business with two departments, state and federal. When you read a case, first determine which "department" it comes from, state or federal. Just like accounting takes care of accounting matters and marketing takes care of marketing matters, federal courts take care of federal matters (federal questions, like violation of the Federal American With Disabilities Act), and state courts take care of state matters (state questions, like violation of the Illinois Disabilities Act). Usually, it is easy to tell whether a matter belongs in federal or state court simply by determining whose law is in question. Is the plaintiff claiming defendant violated a state or federal law?

Sometimes, however, the lines between federal and state, like the lines between accounting and marketing, blur. Suppose that in addition to accounting matters, the accounting department also resolves disputes between different people in the marketing department. In other words, if Pei Pei and Charlene disagreed (who both work in marketing, but have separate specialties) about a marketing matter, the accounting department might settle the dispute. This is not to say that their boss in marketing couldn't solve the problem, but only that in such a case, an option exists to go to the accounting department to obtain a resolution. The same is true in federal court. If there is a dispute between citizens of two different states (e.g., someone in Wisconsin is suing someone in Illinois about violation of an Illinois law), a federal court can hear the case. This situation is referred to as diversity jurisdiction. To recap:

TIP: Decide what "department" the case is in.

✓ Is this a state court case (there is a state law involved—what is it?)

✓ Is this a federal court case (because either there is a federal law involved OR this is a dispute between two citizens of different states about a state matter)

Divisions of Courts within Each Court System

The Trial Court

Obviously, no small business has two departments without a hierarchy in each department. In other words, not everyone is equal in the accounting department. There are junior accountants, senior accountants, and supervisors. The same can be said of the marketing department. Likewise, within each court system, state and federal, there is a hierarchy. Usually cases begin in the trial courts, where a judge and/or jury hears testimony and argument. At trial court, if there is a judge and jury, the judge is in charge of the law, and the jury is in charge of the facts. Returning to our analogy, in the accounting department, most work begins with the junior accountants. They "crunch" the numbers following a procedure set down by those above them. If a question about the numbers themselves arises, the junior accountant is the one to ask because she was the one who crunched the numbers. Likewise, at trial, the jury hears testimony of witnesses and determines who is credible and who is not. In other words, the jury "finds" facts. It, like the accountant crunching numbers, works with the facts. When you read a case, therefore, and there seems to have been a dispute of fact (e.g., did he or didn't he run the red light), it is the jury that decides the answer.

If the jury finds facts, what does the judge do? Like a senior accountant who determines what accounting methods the firm uses, the judge determines what law applies to a particular matter. Let's say the accountant tells his junior associates to use a certain accounting method. The junior associates crunch the numbers, using the system set up by the accountant. Here is another example: Running the red light. The jury decides whether or not the defendant ran the red light. However, the judge has to tell the jury what law to use in resolving the dispute. She has to evaluate what the rules are and what legal standards govern the matter. She instructs the jury on the law (hence the term "jury instructions"). In this case, she might instruct the jury: "Ladies and gentlemen, the law of this state is that everyone has a duty to obey traffic signals. If someone disobeys a traffic signal and, as a result, causes harm to another, then that person shall be liable in negligence." The jury then takes the law and applies it to the facts in order to decide the case.

In cases where there is no jury at the trial court level (plaintiff can decide to waive the jury), a judge determines both the law and the facts of the case.

> **TIP: Distinguish between facts and law.**
>
> Having decided what "department" the case is in, make sure you know:
> - ✓ The facts of the case (usually the jury decides the facts at the trial court level), and
> - ✓ The law according to the trial judge governing the dispute.

The Appellate Court

What if a party doesn't like a decision made by the trial court? What can she do? She can appeal to a higher court. But what does she appeal, exactly? It is important to know that an entire case cannot be appealed to the appellate court. In other words, a party can't simply state on appeal: "The trial court made a bad decision and it should be reversed." What if you disagree that your client ran the red light? What if you think that the jury decided the facts incorrectly? Let's return to our accounting department. Who actually crunched the numbers? Who researched them, checked them, and double-checked them? The junior accountant, of course. If someone discovers that there is a mistake in the books, the mistake can be one of two possibilities:

a) Factual—the accountant used the wrong numbers in the formula; or

b) Policy—the accountant used the wrong accounting method when crunching the numbers.

The same possibility can be said of trial court decisions. If there is a mistake it's either:

a) Factual—the jury incorrectly found the facts (the client did not run a red light); or

b) Legal—the trial court incorrectly instructed the jury as to the law.

When bringing a case up on appeal, attorneys look for a legal mistake rather than a factual one. In other words, if a lawyer believes that the trial court incorrectly instructed the jury as to the law, it is likely that the decision will be appealed. However, if the lawyer believes that the jury incorrectly found the facts (the light was not red, it was green), she will not jump at the chance to appeal. Why? Because in order to overturn findings of fact, the lawyer must prove with clear and convincing evidence that the facts were wrong. This is a very high standard and is rarely established.

Therefore, when reading an appellate case, look for the legal issue on appeal. What, according to the lawyer, was the trial court's legal mistake?

TIP: Dissect the opinion.

✓ Isolate the legal issue on appeal (What mistake of law did the trial court supposedly make?)

✓ Focus on the arguments made by each side. What is the correct statement of law according to the plaintiff? Why is this correct? What is the correct statement of law according to the defendant? Why is this correct?

✓ Evaluate the court's opinion. What is the correct statement of law according to the appellate court? Why did it reject one side's arguments and accept the other's?

What Can the Appellate Court Do with the Trial Court Decision?

If an employee makes a mistake, his boss has several options. She can overturn the employee's decision outright, or she can yell at the employee and tell him to re-do the particular task. In other words, our accountant boss can:

1) decide that her accountants were using the wrong method and overturn the method outright; or

2) decide that her accountants were using the wrong method and tell the employee's to re-crunch the numbers using the new method.

Appellate courts have similar options. They can reverse the trial court's decision altogether. They could also reverse and remand the case back to the trial court for what amounts to a "do-over." Appellate courts are more likely to reverse if there is a pure question of law to consider, such as whether violating a traffic signal is automatic proof of negligence. Appellate courts are more likely to remand if there is a factual component to the decision, such as when, given the correct statement of the law, the trial court needs to go back and consider more facts. Like the accounting department, appellate courts deal with errors in two ways:

1) overturn the lower court decision (i.e., decide that the trial court misconstrued the law); or

2) reverse the prior decision (i.e., decide that the trial court misconstrued the law) and remand the case for further proceedings (i.e., trial court has to re-assess the facts in light of this new standard).

TIP: Isolate the conclusion.

Decide what the appellate court did (reverse, remand, affirm) and why. What was right (or wrong) about the trial court's decision?

Most of the cases you will be reading will be Appellate Court cases. Others will be Supreme Court cases. Therefore, you will not be exploring the facts as much as you will be taking on the law. In other words, at these higher rungs of the court ladder, questions revolve around what the law is concerning an issue rather than the facts in that particular case. This limited reading leaves many students cold because of the lack of the human component in the reading. Because the appellate and supreme courts focus on law instead of facts, you will not explore what each witness had to say in the case, what the effect of the matter was on the plaintiff and defendant, or what the trial court's ruling meant to either side. Instead, you are left with the rather esoteric, and non-dramatic discussion of "the law." Focus on the law and try to understand how and why the court ultimately decided the way it did. Once you have this information you can intelligently discuss different fact scenarios (hypotheticals) and the application of the law to each. In these discussions you can delve into the facts and whether or not the result is good or bad given the circumstances (the human component).

Learning the Language

One of the reasons law students have such a hard time reading and understanding cases is that they don't know the language. Have you ever been to a foreign country and tried to order a meal from a menu in a language that you did not understand? Something as simple as ordering a burger and fries becomes a puzzle. The same phenomenon occurs when new students enter law school and are assigned their first case. Professors assume that students both know what a case is and understand the language the court uses (plaintiff, defendant, replevin, reversed and remanded, etc.). Although students may be familiar with some of the terminology, usually if they do not know the legal meaning of even one word, they blindly end up far from where they were headed. (Like hopping a train to Portland, Maine, instead of Portland, Oregon, or getting a rare steak when you ordered a well-done burger.) You can prevent this from happening to you by following one simple tip: get a good law dictionary and look up every single word or phrase you do not understand. Black's Law Dictionary is a sound investment. This is simple and mundane, but it works. Oftentimes, in a haste to "be done with it," students cut corners. This may mean skipping words they do not understand in the hope that their meaning will magically appear later in the reading, perhaps through context clues. This is not a reliable method in reading cases because it hardly ever happens. To make sure that you know enough language to order from the menu (so to speak), a short dictionary of common legal terms used so often in cases that you should know them is included in the back of this book.

law dictionary

Reading Tips and Techniques

Most law students will admit (or claim) that the bulk of their time is spent reading cases. In fact, one law student admitted that she spent so much time reading and re-reading cases that she had no time for anything else. The good news is that reading cases will help you prepare for class and, ultimately, learn to think like a lawyer. The bad news, though, is that if all you do is read cases, you probably will not do your best on exams. The key is to develop a sensible balance between case reading and the other things you have to do, like synthesizing your notes, outlining, and reviewing. In order to allow sufficient time for all the other things, you have to be able to read cases efficiently. In order to help students use their time more efficiently, we developed the following techniques for reading cases.

Step 1—Anchor yourself.

Never read a case without knowing the context. **Before** you read a case, you need to know what the case is all about. Think of this step as reading a travel guide before you book your trip. Before you read any case, you must do two things: (1) figure out the main issue, which is your anchor; and (2) read an additional source that will give you some general knowledge about that issue.

First, consult the casebook table of contents or the course syllabus to figure out what topic or issue the case will address and **where** this case fits into the big picture. The table of contents may lead you to a main issue and an element or sub-issue. See the sample syllabus.

reading cases

Sample Syllabus

Torts
Fall 2000 Syllabus
Professor Taylor

Office hours
...
Rules and Regulations
...
Assignments
    Intentional Torts
        Battery
            Intent
                Vosburg v. Putney p. 2
                Garratt v. Brown p. 7
            ...
            Harmful or Offensive contact
            ...
    Negligence
    ...
    Strict Liability
    ...

Here, if you are assigned to read the *Vosburg* and *Garratt* cases, you know that you are reading about intentional torts, specifically battery. You also should note that these cases are about the intent element of battery; therefore, intent is your anchor.

Once you have an idea of which issue to look for in the case (intent) and where this topic fits into all of the topics, you will study this term and consult an outside source that will give you some general knowledge about both battery and intent. Here, law school hornbooks, such as *Prosser on Torts*,[3] or commercial outlines, such as *Emanuel Law School Outlines*,[4] can be helpful. These books are very much like the books you read in college in that they are descriptive texts. They define and describe a concept and include the rules that you must extract from your cases.

Commercial outlines, running between $30 and $40 each, are less expensive than hornbooks, and tend to be very general and include few cases. Whatever they are, they are good for giving you an idea of the "big picture" and helping you see the forest, not just the trees. The better outlines (Emanuels and the Example and Explanation series by Aspen) are also good for providing sample exams with answers so that you can test yourself. Hornbooks and treatises, generally starting at $75 each, are more expensive but tend to be more detailed and include extensive footnotes to cases and law review articles that will further explain a topic. Before you spend any money purchasing either, see if your law school has an Academic Support or Academic Assistance office to recommend any study aids to assist you. Also, check with your professor to see which hornbook he or she recommends. By reading a hornbook or commercial outline before

case briefing

reading the case, you gain a general understanding of the topic that the case will address and arm yourself with an anchor that will make case reading easier to understand and quicker to get through.

Step 2—Read the case—focus on your anchor.   *2)*

Once you have your anchor (the topic that the case is about) and you know a bit about the anchor, you can begin reading the case. As you read, focus on the following: (1) the facts, (2) your anchor, and (3) the rule. First you should focus on the facts and try to determine "what happened." You need a factual basis for actions that took place to figure out whether the court found those actions legal or illegal. Second, you should focus on your anchor.

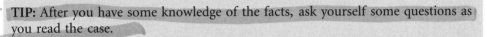

TIP: After you have some knowledge of the facts, ask yourself some questions as you read the case.

- ✓ What does this case tell me about this issue (anchor)?
- ✓ Is the court explaining the issue?
- ✓ Is it dividing the issue into elements or explaining one of the elements?
- ✓ Finally, try to figure out the rule that the court has articulated. In trying to determine the rule, again focus on the anchor. Try to determine whether the court is creating a new rule, rejecting an old rule, or explaining or re-defining an existing rule. After reading the case a couple of times and trying to understand what the case is all about, you are ready to brief the case.

Step 3—Brief the case.   *3)*
What Is a Case Brief?

A case brief is more than a summary of the case. It is a reduction of the case to its essential components that you will need later for class discussion, to create an outline, and to be able to apply the rule to a new set of facts (hypothetical or examination).

Why Should I Brief My Cases?

Case briefs serve three important purposes: they help prepare you for class, they provide an opportunity to practice legal writing, and, along with your class notes, they make a solid foundation for your outline, which you will need to prepare for your final exam.

Class Preparation

By not only reading the case but also briefing it, you will gain a greater understanding of the case and be ready to discuss it in class. Because most law school professors use a modified version of the Socratic method,[5] class preparation is key. Professors expect you to have cases briefed, understand the facts, and are willing and able to explain and expand upon the decision of the court.

Legal Writing

Briefing gets you into the practice of writing in the format expected on exams. When you brief, you learn how to isolate an issue, articulate the legal rules involved, express the court's reasoning in solving the problem the way it did, and pinpoint the conclusion, all in a condensed fashion. All of these skills are crucial for performing well on the exam. You will be expected to isolate the issue, articulate the legal rules, express the reasoning, and come to a conclusion. The more cases you brief and the more often you brief, the more likely it is that you will do well on the exam.

Foundation for Outlining

By briefing each case and subsequently "correcting" your brief during and even after class,[6] you will have most of the information you need to create an outline. Your outline will help you answer the questions on the final exam more effectively.

Briefing Tips and Techniques—FIRAC

How do you brief? Everyone has his own style. You will find that in many law schools, legal writing professors declare that there are 5, 7, or even 9 parts to a brief, but there is no one "right" way to brief. That being said, you will notice that if you compare briefing styles, they all have common components: facts, issue, rule application and conclusion, FIRAC.

1) Write down the name of the case—Use only the last names of the parties (e.g., Miller v. Jones). Do not write down the citation.

2) Summarize the relevant facts of the case—Focus on the "just the facts ma'am" aspect of the case, rather than the procedural details.[7] Although the procedural details might be important to some professors for class discussion, on the exam, you will not be tested on your knowledge of where a case has been or how it got there (unless the course is Civil Procedure). Instead, zero in on what are called the substantive relevant facts. In other words, give the story behind the case. Place yourself in the shoes of the attorney in this case, who is charged with the task of explaining the facts to the jury. How would you summarize what happened? Use the journalistic formula: who did what to whom, where, when, and how?

Substantive Relevant Facts:

Ms. Samson **(who)**, owner of a dog, Spot, **(who)** had him on a leash as she walked to a vacant lot **(where)** on a Saturday morning. **(when)** The lot had

> been owned by the City, but private interests recently have disputed the City's ownership. As Ms. Samson approached the lot, she took Spot off his leash and let him play ball. **(how did this happen)** Spot saw another dog on a leash approaching the lot with its owner, Mr. White. **(whom)** Spot attacked the other dog **(did what)** and scratched Mr. White **(to whom)**. Ms. Samson is charged with violating the City's leash law.

Notice that the facts in a brief do not contain every single detail (i.e., the day of the week, the name of the park or street, the breed of the dogs). Instead, the fact section focuses on the essence of the case. Remember, we are concerned only with who did what to whom, where, when, and how.

3) Isolate the issue—In one question, state the problem that the court has been asked to solve. The issue usually involves a question of law and/or fact. Students tend to make the issue either too specific or too general. In the dog problem, for example, here are some possibilities:

Issue possibility	Problem
Whether Ms. Samson violated the City's leash law ordinance, 123 ILCS 435, when Spot attacked another dog.	**Too specific**—the parties' names do not matter, nor does the citation of the statute. Further, the issue as stated here does not summarize the essence of the dispute.
Whether a person violates a law when a dog attacks another dog.	**Way too general**—"person" does not describe the owner's relationship to the dog; "law" does not focus on the leash law; "another dog" disregards that another dog's owner was also involved.
Whether a dog owner violates a leash law, which mandates that all dogs be on leashes in public places, when the owner has the dog on a leash but drops the leash and allows her dog to run around in a vacant lot, whose ownership between City and private interests is in dispute.	**Just right**—describes, rather than names, the parties: "dog owner" is more specific than "person" but not as specific as "Ms. Samson;" the statute is described rather than identified by number; and the essence of the problem is isolated—a dog is on a leash but the leash is dropped, and the nature of the lot is disputed.

How do you get the issue "just right?" Use the following formula:

WHETHER + SVO + WHEN + FACTS

S V O = Subject Verb Object (verb must be legally significant)

Let's go through the formula:[8]

S = SUBJECT. Describe the subject of the sentence. Remember to keep it descriptive. Rather than name names (Ms. Samson) or generalize (person, plaintiff), you want to describe the parties in a way that indicates their relationship. In this case, "dog owner" is a good description.

V = VERB. The subject must have done something that caused legal consequence. The verb should indicate both the action and the legal consequence. Again, you want to strike a balance between being overly specific (e.g., violated the City's leash law ordinance, 123 ILCS 435) and being overly general (e.g., violated a law). Description is key. In this case, we can describe the subject's action and legal consequence with "violated the City's leash law." This phrase describes the essence of the dispute (the City's leash law). In all cases, you need to balance the over-generalized (e.g., "violated the law") against the overly specific (e.g., "breached Illinois law 124 ILCS 333"), and find something just right ("made an offer for purposes of a contract," or "owed a duty in negligence").

O = OBJECT. If in the "s" of the issue statement, you described the actor, here you will describe the recipient of that action. In other words, you described the actor as a "dog owner." Who was on the receiving end of her action? Not "the defendant" (too general) or "Mr. White" (too specific), but rather "another dog owner."

WHEN + FACTS. After isolating the actors and the action, you need to describe the factual setting. Again, you must strike a balance between the overly specific (e.g., when they met at 156 East Jackson Street, a vacant lot whose ownership is in dispute) and the overly general (when one dog ran after another dog). Ask yourself, "What facts in this case make this a difficult problem to solve?" In this case, it is both the leash situation (technically leashed but running around) and the nature of the lot (ownership in dispute). Both of these FACTS will make our analysis of the elements "leashed" and "public property" difficult; therefore, we must list both in our issue. Remember, you need to include FACTS, not legal conclusions at this point.

Example:

> **Do say:** ... when the owner has the dog on a leash but drops the leash and allows her dog to run around in a vacant lot, whose ownership between City and private interests is in dispute. [The phrase is factual (dog is on a leash but leash is dropped, lot ownership is in dispute) without being overly specific.]

> **Don't say:** ... when the dog is not leashed and the property is public. [This phrase describes legal conclusions. The term "leashed" in this context is a legal conclusion, which is in dispute—we do not know if the dog is "leashed" according to the statute until we know what the City law means by "leashed." Likewise, whether the property is public is a legal conclusion that is in dispute; what does "public" mean—owned by the City? Can a property whose ownership is in dispute be called "public?"]

4) Articulate the rules—State the rule(s) of law that the court used to solve the issue. Rules can come from either statutes or cases. Remember, a rule is a statement of the law that proscribes what a person can or cannot do under certain circumstances. Even though the court may discuss many rules in making its decision, focus on the rules that relate to the issue. For example, in the negligence problem, focus on the rules that relate to reasonable duty of care. Paraphrase the rules. It is not always necessary to write down the case they came from; what matters is that you pinpoint the rule (e.g., When one breaches the duty of reasonable care to another, one is negligent. The duty of rea-

sonable care is determined by considering whether a reasonable person, if put in the defendant's situation, would have acted in a similar manner).

Any given case may have many rules. Focus on only those rules that relate to your
issue. In other words, if the issue is what constitutes "intent" for purposes of battery,
then the only rules to note are those dealing with the "intent" element of battery. In our
dog example, the rules that you must brief are those that relate to the City leash law—
what the law says and how prior decisions have interpreted the terms "leashed" and
"public." Has any previous case dealt with these interpretations? Remember, we are trying to see how the court solved Ms. Samson's problem. Before deciding her case, the
court turns to prior decisions for guidance, much like any human being making a decision about her life seeks others for advice. Perhaps previous definitions and interpretations will help this court decide this case.

5) **Begin the application**—Also known as the reasoning, rationale, or analysis, the application is often described as the "why" of the case. In this section, you must determine why the court decided the way it did. The application section may have as many
as three parts.

Main—The main argument. Why did the court say a certain party should win the dispute? Here you should strive to combine the rules and the facts. In other words, the
main argument should not simply repeat either the facts or the law. Instead, you should
show how the court combined the rules and the facts of this particular situation.

Example:

Don't say: The court cited previous cases in which a dog was leashed, meaning
the owner maintained a hold on the other end, and public, meaning city-
owned. [There are no facts, only regurgitation of the rules without any indication of HOW these rules helped the court solve this problem.]

Don't say: Here the dog was on a leash, which the owner had dropped, and the
lot was vacant. [There are no rules, only regurgitation of the facts without any
indication of how the facts and the law worked together to solve this problem
does not help solve our problem.]

Do say: As to the word "leashed," the court cited a previous decision that con-
strued that word to mean "connected to owner." In this case, because the leash
was not in Ms. Samson's hand, Spot was not "leashed" pursuant to the statute.
As to the term "public," the court found previous decisions holding that "public" means "owned by a public entity," such as a city. In this case, because the
ownership of the lot is in dispute, the court could not say it was public, in the
sense that the lot is vacant (and, therefore, not held out to the public) and there
is no indication as to the ownership of the property from just looking at it. [No-
tice how the rules blend with the law to form the application. In this section,
you need to show how the court used the rules to solve a new and different
problem.]

TIP: To ensure that you are completing the application section fully, count the
number of times you use the word "because" in your answer. "Because" should be
the bridge between the rule ("leashed" means "connected to owner") and the

facts (Ms. Samson was not holding Spot's leash). Also, highlight all the facts in yellow and all the rules in pink. Stand back and look at the application. Is it all pink? If so, you have too many rules. Is it all yellow? If so, you have too many facts. Is it pink on top and yellow on the bottom? If so, you have isolated but not integrated rules and facts.

Example:

Application — too many facts

> **Here the dog was on a leash that the owner had dropped and the lot was vacant.**

Application — all rules, no facts

> The court cited previous cases where a dog was "leashed" meaning the owner was on the other end, and "public" meaning city-owned.

Application — rules and facts isolated

> The court cited previous cases where a dog was "leashed" meaning the owner was on the other end, and "public" meaning city-owned. **Here, the dog was on a leash that the owner had dropped and the lot was vacant.**

Application — good mix of rules and facts

> As to the term "leashed," the court cited a previous decision that construed that phrase to mean "connected to owner." **In this case, because the leash was not in Ms. Samson's hand, Spot was not** "leashed" pursuant to the statute. As to the term "public," the court found previous decisions holding that public means "owned by a public entity," such as a city. **In this case, because the ownership of the lot is in dispute,** the court could not say it was public, **in the sense that the lot is vacant** (and therefore not held out to the public) **and there is no indication as to the character of the property from just looking at it.**

Opposing — The argument made by the other party or by the dissenting judge. Focus on the arguments made for the other side in terms of the law and the facts combined, just as you did in the main argument. For example, "Ms. Samson did not violate the leash law because Spot was leashed in the sense that he had on a dog collar and a leash; Ms. Samson merely let go temporarily. Thus, this was not a situation in which the dog was running around completely loose. She could have picked up the leash and restrained Spot at any time."

Rebuttal — The reasons why the opposing arguments fail. Focus on the weakness of the opposing arguments and explain why the correct conclusion goes back to the main argument. For example, "Ms. Samson's argument that her dog was 'leashed' fails. Contrary to her assertion, Spot was not 'leashed' in the sense that she could pick up the leash and restrain him at any time, because the very fact that she was unable to do so when Mr. White came along belies this contention of control."

6) Don't forget the conclusion — A direct and complete answer to the issue, sometimes called "the holding," this is what the court ultimately decided. For example, "Although Ms. Samson did not have her dog leashed pursuant to the City's leash law, the dog was not on 'public' land (because of the ownership dispute) and, therefore, she was not in violation of the statute."

TIP: A good brief should give you a sense of déjà vu all over again. Make sure:

✓ All the facts in the **fact** section reappear in the **application** section and vice versa. If there are facts in the fact section that you didn't use in the application, they are either (1) irrelevant, or (2) you forgot to use them in the application. If you have facts in the application section that do not appear in the fact section, you forgot to brief them in the fact section.

✓ The **issue** should combine part of the rule briefed in the **rule** section (in the V of SVO) and the pertinent **facts** briefed in the fact section (when …).

✓ The **rule** should be foreshadowed in the **issue** and incorporated into the **application**.

✓ The **application** (as illustrated in the yellow and pink exercise) should combine both the **facts** (briefed in the fact section) and the **rules** (briefed in the rule section).

✓ The **conclusion**, like the issue, should also be a combination of **fact** and **rule**.

These techniques for reading and briefing cases should help you to prepare more effectively for class and succeed in extracting the rule from the cases. Below we have provided a case and a sample brief using the FIRAC method, along with an exercise to help you practice the skill of reading and briefing cases.

Sample Case and Case Brief

Vosburg v. Putney[9]
80 Wis. 523, 50 N.W. 403 (1891)

Lyon, J.

[The plaintiff, 14 years old at the time in question, brought an action for battery against the defendant, 12 years old. The complaint charged that the defendant kicked the plaintiff in the shin in a schoolroom in Waukesha, Wisconsin, after the teacher had called the class to order. The kick aggravated a prior injury that the plaintiff had suffered and caused his leg to become lame. The jury found, in a special verdict, that plaintiff had, during the month of January 1889, received an injury just above the knee, which became inflamed and produced pus and that such injury had, on February 20, 1889, nearly healed at the point of the injury. The jury further found that the plaintiff had not, prior to February 20, been lame as a result of such injury, nor had his tibia in his right leg become inflamed or diseased to some extent before he received the blow or kick from the defendant. Instead, it was the defendant's kick that was the exciting cause of the injury to the plaintiff's leg. And, although the defendant, in touching the plaintiff with his foot, did not intend to do plaintiff any harm, the jury awarded plaintiff twenty-five hundred dollars. The trial court entered judgment for the plaintiff on the special verdict and the defendant appealed.]

The jury having found that the defendant, in touching the plaintiff with his foot, did not intend to do him any harm, counsel for defendant maintains that the plaintiff has no cause of action, and that the defendant's motion for judgment on the special verdict should have been granted. In support of his proposition, counsel quotes from 2 Greenl. Ev. 83, the rule that "the intention to do harm is of the essence of an assault." Such is the rule, no doubt, in actions or prosecutions for mere assaults. But this is an action to recover damages for an alleged assault and battery. In such cases, the rule is correctly stated, in many of the authorities cited by counsel that plaintiff must show either that the intention was unlawful or that the defendant intended the act itself, even if he did not intend the subsequent harm. If the intended act is unlawful, the intention to commit it must necessarily be unlawful. Hence, as applied to this case, kicking the plaintiff by the defendant was an unlawful act, and the defendant desired to kick plaintiff. Had the parties been upon the playgrounds of the school, engaged in the usual boyish sports, the defendant being free from malice, wantonness, or negligence, and intending no harm to plaintiff in what he did, we should hesitate to hold the act of the defendant unlawful or that he could be held liable in this action. Some consideration is due to the implied license of the playgrounds. But it appears that the injury was inflicted in the school, after it had been called to order by the teacher and after the regular exercises of the school had commenced. Under these circumstances, no implied license to do the act complained of existed, and such act was a violation of the order and decorum of the school and necessarily unlawful. In addition, although the defendant might not have intended the plaintiff to become lame, there is no question that he intended to kick him. One who intends the act is also responsible for the subsequent harm. Hence, we are of the opinion that, under the evidence and verdict, the action may be sustained.

Sample Case Brief

NAME: *Vosburg v. Putney*

FACTS: Two boys were in a classroom during school hours; the class had just been called to order by the teacher. The defendant kicked the plaintiff in the shin. Afterward, the shin area became infected, and the plaintiff eventually lost use of his limb.

ISSUE: Whether a boy satisfied the intent element of battery when he kicked another boy in the knee (while in class) and, as a result, the knee later became infected and diseased and the boy became lame.

RULE: In an action to recover damages for an alleged assault and battery, the plaintiff must show either that the defendant intended to do the act and the act was unlawful or that the defendant intended the ultimate result. If the intended act is unlawful, then the intention to commit it must necessarily be unlawful.

APPLICATION: Here, the boy did not intend the end result (injuring his friend's leg so severely), but he did intend to kick him in the shin during a time (class in session) and a place where (the classroom) this action (the kicking) was unlawful. Because he intended the act (kicking) and the kick was unlawful, he satisfied the intent element of battery.

CONCLUSION: Yes. Because the defendant's intended act of kicking the plaintiff was unlawful, his intention to kick plaintiff was also unlawful. Defendant is responsible for any harm resulting from his unlawful act.

Exercise

Exercise 3-1
Reading and Briefing Cases

Please read the following case and prepare a case brief. Please refer back to the sample class syllabus provided in this chapter prior to reading this case.

Garratt v. Dailey

279 P.2d 1091 (Wis. 1955)

The liability of an infant for an alleged battery is presented to this court for the first time. Brian Dailey (age five years, nine months) was visiting with Naomi Garratt, an adult and a sister of the plaintiff, Ruth Garratt, likewise an adult, in the backyard of the plaintiff's home on July 16, 1951. It is plaintiff's contention that she came out into the backyard to talk with Naomi and that, as she started to sit down in a wood and canvas lawn chair, Brian deliberately pulled it out from under her.... The trial court, unwilling to accept this testimony, adopted instead Brian Dailey's version of what happened, and made the following findings:

"III. ... [W]hile Naomi Garratt and Brian Dailey were in the back yard, the plaintiff, Ruth Garratt, came out of her house into the back yard. Some time subsequent thereto, defendant, Brian Dailey, picked up a lightly built wood and canvas lawn chair which was then and there located in the back yard of the above-described premises, moved it sideways a few feet and seated himself therein, at which time, he discovered the plaintiff, Ruth Garratt, about to sit down at the place where the lawn chair had formerly been, at which time, he hurriedly got up from the chair and attempted to move it toward Ruth Garratt to aid her in sitting down in the chair; that due to the defendant's small size and lack of dexterity, he was unable to get the lawn chair under the plaintiff in time to prevent her from falling to the ground. Plaintiff fell to the ground and sustained a fracture of her hip, and other injuries and damages as hereinafter set forth.

It is urged that Brian's action in moving the chair constituted a battery. A definition (not all-inclusive but sufficient for our purpose) of a battery is the intentional infliction of a harmful bodily contact upon another. The rule that determines liability for battery is given in 1 Restatement, Torts, 29, §13, as: "An act which, directly or indirectly, is the legal cause of a harmful contact with another's person makes the actor liable to the other, if (a) the act is done with the intention of bringing about a harmful or offensive contact or an apprehension thereof to the other or a third person, and (b) the contact is not consented to by the other or the other's consent thereto is procured by fraud or duress, and (c) the contact is not otherwise privileged."

We have in this case no question of consent or privilege. We, therefore, proceed to an immediate consideration of intent and its place in the law of battery. In the comment on clause (a), the Restatement says: "Character of actor's intention. In order that an act may be done with the intention of bringing about a harmful or offensive contact or an apprehension thereof to a particular person, either the other or a third person, the act must be done for the purpose of causing the contact or apprehension or with knowledge on the part of the actor that such contact or apprehension is substantially certain to be produced." See also Prosser on Torts 41, §8. We have here the conceded volitional act of Brian, i.e., the moving of a chair. Had the plaintiff proved to the satisfaction of the trial court that Brian moved the chair while she was in the act of sitting down, Brian's action would patently have been for the purpose or with the intent of causing the plaintiff's bodily contact with the ground, and she would be entitled to a judgment against him for the resulting damages. *Vosburg v. Putney* (1891), 80 Wis. 523, 50 N. W. 403; *Briese v. Maechtle*, supra. After the trial court determined that the plaintiff had not established her theory of a battery (i.e., that Brian had pulled the chair out from under the plaintiff while she was in the act of sitting down), it then became concerned whether a battery was established under the facts as it found them to be. A battery would be established if, in addition to plaintiff's fall, it was proved that, when Brian moved the chair, he knew with substantial certainty that the plaintiff would attempt to sit down where the chair had been.... The mere absence of any intent to injure the plaintiff or to play a prank on her or to embarrass her, or to commit an assault and battery on her would not absolve him from liability if, in fact, he had such knowledge. *Mercer v. Corbin* (1889), 117 Ind. 450, 20 N. E. 132, 3 L. R. A. 221. Without such knowledge, there would be nothing wrongful about Brian's act in moving the chair, and, there being no wrongful act, there would be no liability.

While a finding that Brian had no such knowledge can be inferred from the findings made, we believe that before the plaintiff's action in such a case should be dismissed, there should be no question that the trial court had passed upon that issue; hence, the case should be remanded for clarification of the findings to specifically cover the question of Brian's knowledge because intent could be inferred therefrom. If the court finds that he had such knowledge, the necessary intent will be established, and the plaintiff will be entitled to recover, even though there was no purpose to injure or embarrass the plaintiff. *Vosburg v. Putney*, supra. If Brian did not have such knowledge, there was no wrongful act by him, and the basic premise of liability on the theory of a battery was not established.

Answer to Exercise 3-1
Sample Case Brief

NAME: *Garratt v. Dailey*

FACTS: Five-year old boy (Dailey) moved a chair from under an adult as she started to sit down. Adult claimed that the boy deliberately pulled chair out from under her. Trial court accepted boy's version of facts. According to Dailey, he originally moved the chair and sat in it himself, but when he noticed that plaintiff was about to sit down where the chair had been, he tried to put the chair under the adult. Unfortunately, he wasn't able to place the chair in the right place in time.

ISSUE: Did Dailey have the requisite intent for battery when he allegedly removed a chair from the place where an adult was about to sit down, and the adult fell and suffered injuries?

RULES: Battery is the intentional infliction of harmful contact upon the body of another. In order to satisfy the intent requirement, plaintiff must prove that the act was done with the intention of bringing about a harmful or offensive contact or an apprehension of a harmful or offensive contact (absent consent or privilege). In other words, the act must have been done for the purpose of causing the contact, or done with the actor's knowledge that such contact or apprehension was **substantially certain** to occur.

APPLICATION: In this case, the trial court determined that the plaintiff failed to prove that Dailey pulled the chair out while she was in the act of sitting down. Thus, it cannot be said that the act was done for the purpose of causing the contact; however, it is unclear whether Dailey knew that such contact was **substantially certain** to occur. Plaintiff would establish a battery if, in addition to her fall, she proved that Dailey **knew with substantial certainty** when he moved the chair that she would attempt to sit down where the chair had been. The mere absence of an intent to injure the plaintiff, to play a prank on her, to embarrass her, or to commit an assault and battery on her would not absolve Dailey from liability if, in fact, he had such **knowledge**.

CONCLUSION: Unclear whether Dailey possessed the intent to commit a battery when he removed a chair from the place where an adult was about to sit down, and the adult sat down, fell, and suffered injuries. Case remanded to determine whether Dailey, when he moved the chair, knew **with substantial certainty** that plaintiff would sit down where the chair had been.

Endnotes

1. Cases are first heard in a trial court, and if one of the parties disputes the result, the case then goes to an appellate court for review. For more information on the court system and the life of a case see Dale A. Nancy, *Law and Justice*, 214, 227 (2nd ed. 1998).

2. Ira Shafiroff, *Essay Writing Super Seminar*, Sum and Substance (2nd ed. 1998).

3. W. Page Keeton, *Prosser and Keeton on the Law of Torts* (5th ed. 1984).

4. Steven Emanuel, *Contracts Law Outline* (1995).

5. For a more detailed analysis of the Socratic and Langdellian Method, see Chapter 1.

6. *See* Chapter 3 on Notetaking for more information on how to use your case briefs during class.

7. The procedural facts tell how this case got to this particular court. Did the case go to trial and get dismissed? Was the case decided at trial and did the losing party appeal to this court?

8. The SVO formula is taken from Richard Wydick, *Plain English for Lawyers* (4th ed. 1998).

9. This case has been modified from its original form.

Chapter 4

Effective Notetaking in Law School

As explained earlier, once you have gained context (*i.e.*, you know where you've been and where you're going), you are ready to develop the first critical law school skill — the ability to extract rules from a series of cases. Unfortunately, there is no "book of laws" in American jurisprudence. No one book collects and organizes all the laws of the land in one convenient source. Instead, our system of law revolves around cases. Each court develops, interprets and sometimes changes the law in any given area. Thus, it is critical to develop the ability to extract the rules from a variety of sources. In a way, you are putting together your own book of laws for any given course; you are extracting the general rules and exceptions for yourself.

Some students feel that, in the end, they end up teaching themselves the course. In a way, this is true. It is not necessarily true that law professors don't teach you anything at all. They just teach in a manner that is very different from what you may have experienced in the past. Before we explore what notes you should take in law school, let's explore the difference between notes in college and notes in law school.

Difference Between Notes in College and Notes in Law School

You may remember getting writer's cramp in college from attempting to write down every single word that came out of the professor's mouth. After that, you soon realized that a tape recorder would work much better and that you could listen to the professor's lecture over and over again until the information sank in. In a pure lecture class, writing down all or most of what is said is important. Because the professor tells you exactly what you need to know, you can memorize and repeat this information on the exam and do well in the class. The same is not true for law school. You may need to memorize the rules for an exam; however, you certainly will not need to memorize every single fact of every case, or everything that was said during every class session. As we mentioned earlier in Chapter 1, law school is very different from college. You need to understand the problem solving process that takes place in each case you read, so that you can apply that method to a new fact pattern on the exam. In that respect, you are not expected to memorize all the professor's words; rather, you must focus on the law and the application of the law in class. Your notes should reflect this goal.

Dos and Don'ts for Taking Notes

We offer the following information with this **caveat:** this is not the only method for taking notes. You may talk to other law students who take more or fewer notes, and take them in different ways, and still do very well in law school. Our purpose here is to provide you with a template or a starting point to help you focus on the important information during class discussion. We do not want you to become frustrated or overwhelmed at the amount of information you will learn in law school. Accordingly, we offer the following suggestions when taking notes.

First, don't write down everything the professor and other students say. Remember: this is not college. You are not required to regurgitate, word for word, the professor's brilliant speeches. You are required to use the information to solve new problems.

Second, don't space out and not take a single note. One year, we had a student who did not do very well his first semester. We observed him in class, where he spent most of his time reading his cases. He didn't take a single note during the entire fifty minutes! Class time should be used for listening to the dialogue and understanding the cases. Although you do not want a verbatim transcript, you also do not want a blank sheet of paper at the end of class. Remember: you need to use your notes to guide you in examination preparation because they will help you identify which issues are important to your professor.

Third, try to separate the relevant information from the irrelevant. What is relevant? Think back to FIRAC—fact, issue, rule, application, and conclusion. You should continually focus on FIRAC as your problem solving technique for each case you read. We suggest you take notes in three general categories: (1) editing your case briefs, (2) writing down hypotheticals and examples (*i.e.*, application of rule), and (3) writing down other relevant "stuff" (social policy, dissent, theories, etc.).

Edit Your Brief

During class, most professors will start with questions on cases assigned for that class. She will ask for the facts of the case, the holding, and the reasoning. During this process, the professor is trying to teach you the legal problem solving method. She is trying to help you understand the facts of the case, the issue, the rule, the application of that rule, and the conclusion—FIRAC. During class time, you should correct your case brief. Remember: your brief is **your** attempt to understand how the court solved the issue in that case. Your first order of business should be to check your brief for mistakes. Make sure that you are dissecting each case properly; therefore, you need to check for each part of FIRAC.

Checklist for IRAC

TIP: Use this checklist for your brief:

✓ Did you include the relevant facts?

✓ Did you have too many facts or not enough?

✓ Did you get the correct issue?

✓ Does your issue statement combine the legal issue with the relevant facts?

✓ Did you correctly articulate the rule?

✓ Was your statement of the rule worded **exactly** as the professor wants?

✓ Did you correctly identify the court's rationale (and understand the application)?

Write Down All Hypotheticals

After discussing a case, your professor may change the facts or present a hypothetical situation. If so, write this information down. Hypotheticals ("hypos") are additional examples similar to the facts of the case, usually offered to illustrate some portion of the rule. Hypos demonstrate how to solve similar problems using FIRAC. When the facts change, or when you are given a new set of facts, you need to go through FIRAC to solve the new problem. The issue and the rule may be the same as the one discussed in the case at hand, but the application or reasons why the outcome is the way it is will be different. Hypos and the reasoning or rationale are examples of the application part of FIRAC, and you should write these down to study later for the exam. Again, law school exams do not test your memory of a case inside and out. Instead, they test your ability to take a rule you've learned and apply it to different facts. So when your professor poses hypotheticals, she's doing just that—she's taking the rule you learned in a case and is asking you to apply it to a different set of facts. You should treat hypotheticals like mini-exam questions and write down all hypotheticals.

Note How the "Other Stuff" Relates to FIRAC

You may be thinking, okay, everything so far makes sense, but what do I do with all the "other stuff" that comes up in class? What do I do with the new legal concepts or Latin phrases that my professor keeps mentioning? What about all these other issues like social policy or newspaper articles that the professor discusses? Should I take notes on that information? Absolutely. If your professor mentions something in class that seems off track, you need to ask: "How will this help me on the exam? Will this information contribute to my approach to solving new problems?"

Your professor may discuss topics that seem unrelated to the case. These include topics like social policy, economic concerns (*i.e.*, who pays for what), and jurisdiction (*i.e.*, whether the courts or the legislature should decide this issue). During this discussion, your professor is attempting to point out the broader ramifications of the court's decision. Here the emphasis is not so much on the rules or elements, but rather social pol-

hypotheticals

icy. In these instances, you need to focus on how this relates to FIRAC—how can this information help solve a new legal problem in the future (*i.e.* on the exam)? Does it concern the application of the rule? Should other reasons, besides the facts, make the court decide differently? Think about this information, jot it down, and try to make some connection to FIRAC and the problem solving method.

Legal phrases, what we call "magic words," must be learned and can be helpful later. Some legal concepts, which take many words to explain, can be summed up in a single word or phrase, for example, "proximate cause" or "constructive eviction." When you hear these words or phrases used in class, write them down. These are "magic words." They can be legal terms of art (*res ipsa loquitor*) or terms a professor uses to refer to a concept (victimless crimes). You will get points on the exam if you know what these terms mean and use them correctly.

Finally, some professors begin or end class with a summary of what happened last time. Make sure to write this down. This review will be an invaluable guide to how the professor wants you to analyze a problem and show how it all fits together. Legal analysis is very orderly; you must analyze elements not only separately but also in a certain order. Make sure you know both the elements and the order of analysis.

note tips for class:

> **TIP:** While taking notes in class, make sure you:
>
> ✓ Edit your brief.
> ✓ Write down hypotheticals.
> ✓ Include the magic words.
> ✓ Include the professor's summary.

Now that you have an idea of what to focus on during class discussion, we want to give you a taste of what a law school classroom is like. The following is a transcript of an actual law school class discussion and sample notes taken from that discussion.

Sample Class Discussion

Torts Class Discussion

PROF: Good morning, class. Last week we began our unit on intentional torts and discussed the tort of assault. Today, we're going to talk about its partner in crime: battery. Sarah, who has the burden of proof in a battery case?

SARAH: The plaintiff.

PROF: And what kind of case must the plaintiff make out?

SARAH: A *prima facie* case.

PROF: And what does that mean?

SARAH:	That the facts of the plaintiff's case are good on their face, absent any defenses.
PROF:	Good. On its face, the proof offered by the plaintiff is at least good enough that a judge will not dismiss the claim but allow it to go to trial, so a jury may decide. The defendant may offer any number of defenses, but this won't be necessary if the plaintiff cannot make out a *prima facie* case. Now, Sarah, tell me what the definition of a battery is.
SARAH:	Um … when someone acts intending to cause a harmful or offensive contact against another person that results in that person being harmed.
PROF:	Do you have to actually touch the person?
SARAH:	Yes?
PROF:	Jose, do you have to actually touch the person?
JOSE:	No, you don't actually have to touch the person for the contact to be offensive.
PROF:	What do you have to do?
JOSE:	The contact is offensive if it offends a person's reasonable sense of personal dignity.
PROF:	So if you're wearing a baseball cap, and I come charging at you and knock your hat off of your head, have I just committed a battery?
JOSE:	Yes, because the hat was an extension of my person, and you offended my sense of dignity.
PROF:	Good. Now, let's take a look at today's reading, in which the person didn't even touch an extension of the person's self. Keisha, what were the facts in *Vosburg v. Putney*?
KEISHA:	The defendant kicked the plaintiff in the leg while they were at school.
PROF:	Where were they?
KEISHA:	They were in class.
PROF:	Were they standing up and fighting?
KEISHA:	No, they were sitting in their desks on opposite sides of an aisle, and the defendant kicked the plaintiff from his desk.
PROF:	So what happened after the kick?
KEISHA:	The plaintiff didn't really feel pain at first, but later on, it became inflamed and really began to hurt him.
PROF:	Okay good. Now, what court heard this case?
KEISHA:	The Wisconsin Supreme Court.
PROF:	Good. How did the court know what the facts of the case were?
KEISHA:	The court got the facts from the trial record.
PROF:	Okay, now what if the court thought that the facts—as the trial court found them to be—were more than likely not what really happened? What's the standard of review then?
KEISHA:	The court must accept the facts found at trial unless they are "clearly erroneous."
PROF:	Okay good. Now, why did the plaintiff win in this case?

KEISHA: The defendant intended to kick the plaintiff; it wasn't an accident. That kick caused the harm the plaintiff suffered.

PROF: We'll talk more about this later when we talk about defenses to intentional torts, but why don't you take a stab at it now? Could the defendant raise any defense to his actions?

KEISHA: No, I don't think so. He wasn't defending himself in a fight, so he didn't really have any justification, other than a personal grudge, I guess.

PROF: Good, Keisha. Now, argue the other side. What did the defendant say?

KEISHA: That the kick wasn't that hard, and the plaintiff didn't even feel it. The plaintiff's injuries were not a result of the kick but merely a coincidence.

PROF: Good job. Now, Tim, this was called a "special verdict" because the jury answered specific questions, instead of rendering a verdict in favor of or against liability. What did the jury find with regard to whether the defendant intentionally attempted to hurt the plaintiff?

TIM: The jury found that "the defendant, in touching the plaintiff with his foot," did not intend to do him any harm.

PROF: What was the issue for the Wisconsin Supreme Court?

TIM: The issue was whether the trial court judge should have held in favor of the defendant, because the jury found that he did not intend to inflict the harm the plaintiff suffered.

PROF: And how did the court decide?

TIM: The court held that the trial judge was correct in finding in favor of the plaintiff.

PROF: What legal reasoning did the court use to reach that holding?

TIM: The court held that it was not necessary for the defendant to "intend" to cause the harm. It was sufficient that the defendant intended to perform the unlawful act of kicking the plaintiff.

PROF: Good. And how did the court determine whether the kick was an unlawful act?

TIM: Um ... the court looked at where the kick took place. They said....

PROF: Correction, Tim. You said "they." Even though the court is made up of several judges here, you still refer to the court as a singular entity. So you would say, "it held," not "they held."

TIM: Oh, okay. It held that since the kick took place during school hours, in a classroom, after the teacher had called class to order, the kick was unlawful.

PROF: What if the plaintiff had been kicked while playing outside during recess?

TIM: The court said there may have been some type of "implied license."

PROF: That's correct, but why would there have been such a license?

TIM: Because if the boys had been involved in some sort of game or sport on the playground, the plaintiff would be said to have "assumed the risk."

PROF: That's right. In a situation such as playing a rough game of, say soccer, there is no express license to hurt other players; however, by voluntarily participating in a game in which injury is likely to result, we imply consent to be injured. But as we'll see later, even that defense has its limitations.

MATT: Wait, I'm a little confused. Doesn't the fact that these are kids have anything to do with it?

PROF: Well, how old were the plaintiff and defendant?

MATT: The plaintiff was 14 and the defendant was 12.

PROF: How does that affect the case?

MATT: Um … the defendant was young, so he might not have known what he was doing?

PROF: Well, I think he knew what he was doing. He kicked him in the leg!

MATT: What I meant was that he probably didn't expect to have hurt him so badly just by kicking him in the leg. I mean that he was 2 years younger than the plaintiff and probably smaller, too.

PROF: Does that matter? Twelve years old isn't *that* young.

MATT: Well, he didn't intend to hurt him.

PROF: But that's not the issue. The issue is the act itself. Again, What's the rule for battery?

MATT: Someone who intends to cause a harmful act, and that act results in a harm.

PROF: So if he intended to kick him, and that kick resulted in a harm, is he liable for battery?

MATT: I guess so, yes. But how was he supposed to know that the fourteen-year-old had a problem with his leg?

PROF: He probably didn't, but that doesn't matter either. Remember that you take the plaintiff as he is. Here's a hypo: you're waiting to use a public telephone and you're really in a hurry because this girl you've been wanting to date has just texted you and your battery is low. There's someone else already using the phone. After waiting five minutes, you get impatient and yank him away from the phone. He stumbles backward, trips, and hits his head on the ground. Lo and behold, he has a unique condition called "egg-shell skull syndrome," and he fractures his skull and starts bleeding profusely. Did you know that he had an eggshell skull?

MATT: No, but I suspect it doesn't matter that I didn't intend for him to hit his head and start bleeding.

PROF: Exactly. You intended to pull him away from the phone. As a result of that action, he suffered an injury, and you're liable. Now, let's take that scenario one step further. What if you never touched the person, but as a result of your actions, that person suffered an injury? Jen, let's say that you see Matt walking down the hall. You drop a banana peel on the ground around a corner, right where you know Matt will walk. He slips and breaks his wrist as he falls. Are you liable for battery?

JEN: Um … based on the rule we just learned, I think I am because I knew that he would slip on it. But like the other case, I didn't intend to hurt him, and it's not like I physically pushed him down or anything.

PROF: Well, let's see if that holds true as we continue our look at battery with *Garratt v. Dailey.*

Sample Notes

CAVEATS: Below are sample notes that you might have taken if you attended the class discussion above. Observe how the notes focus on making changes/additions to the case brief, as well as on definitions, hypos and other points that the professor deems important.

Battery

Plaintiff must make out a "prima facie case"—proof offered by the plaintiff is good enough that a judge will not dismiss the claim but will allow it to go to trial so that a jury will decide.

Definition of battery

When someone acts intending to cause harmful or offensive contact against another person that results in that person being harmed. You don't have to actually touch the person for the contact to be offensive—the contact is offensive if it offends a person's reasonable sense of personal dignity.

Hypo #1: Wearing a baseball cap and someone charges at you, hitting you in the head is battery because the hat is an extension of the person, and you have offended her sense of dignity.

Special verdict: when a jury answers one or more specific questions, instead of rendering a verdict regarding liability.

Unlawful act: the court considers special circumstances of the situation. Specifically, this court considered when the alleged activity took place (in the classroom during organized class time).

Implied license: Consent or permission to do an act, implied from the circumstances, other than expressly given, i.e. consent to touching in a soccer game.

Age: In this case, the court was unconcerned whether the children were of a certain age. Instead, it considered whether the child had the ability, not to understand his action would harm another, but the intent to commit an illegal act.

Hypo #2: You are waiting to use the public telephone and you are in a hurry. Someone is already using the phone. After waiting five minutes, you get impatient and yank the phone away from him. He stumbles backwards, trips, and hits his head. Turns out he has a condition known as egg-shell skull syndrome and starts bleeding profusely. This is considered battery because you intended to pull the phone away from him; therefore, you are still liable.

Hypo #3: If you never touched the person, but, as a result of your actions, the person suffered an injury (drop a banana on ground, knowing that someone will likely walk over it and slip and fall), you are liable because you knew that the your action (dropping a banana on ground) would cause harm.

Sample Case Brief

NAME: *Vosburg v. Putney*

FACTS: Two boys were in a classroom during school hours; the class had just been called to order by the teacher. The defendant reached across the aisle with his foot and kicked his toe against the plaintiff's shin. Afterward, the shin area became infected, and the plaintiff eventually became lame.

ISSUE: Whether a boy satisfied the intent element of battery when he kicked another boy in the knee (while in class) and, as a result, the knee later became infected and diseased.

RULE: In an action to recover damages for an alleged assault and battery, the plaintiff must show either that the defendant intended to do the act and the act was unlawful or that the defendant intended the ultimate result. If the intended act is unlawful, then the intention to commit it must necessarily be unlawful.

APPLICATION: Here, the boy did not intend the end result (injuring his friend's leg so severely), but he did intend to kick him in the shin during a time (class in session) and a place (the classroom) where this action (the kicking) was unlawful. Because he intended the act (kicking) and the kick was unlawful, he satisfied the intent element of battery.

CONCLUSION: Yes. Because the defendant's intentional act of kicking the plaintiff was unlawful, his intention to kick plaintiff was also unlawful. Defendant was at fault for any harm resulting from his unlawful act.

Corrections/additions to brief made during class

Relevant facts: In the classroom—called to order—that made kick illegal.

Issue: intent is key

Rule: Battery is committed when one person acts intending to cause harmful or offensive contact against another person that results in that person being harmed. It is also sufficient that a person intends to perform an unlawful act (this is what happened here).

Application/reasoning: The defendant intended to touch the plaintiff in an offensive manner, even though he did not intend to cause him harm. The act of performing the unlawful kick is sufficient to satisfy the intent element for battery. The kick occurred in the classroom, after the teacher had called the class to order. The act was unlawful because it occurred in a place and at a time that kicking is not allowed or lawful.

Conclusion: The defendant committed a battery when he intended to perform an illegal act by kicking the plaintiff during school while class was in session.

More additions to brief:

Procedural history: The trial court found for the plaintiff, even though the defendant did not intend to inflict the harm the plaintiff suffered. The Supreme Court of Wisconsin found that the trial judge was correct in finding in favor of the plaintiff.

TIP: Take five minutes after each class to summarize the day's discussion. Limit yourself to one sentence. For this day's discussion, your one sentence summary should be about intent. How do you know if someone has satisfied the intent element for battery? By taking the time after class, you:

✓ Revisit the class information while it's fresh in your mind, thereby increasing recall and comprehension.

✓ You are able to assess whether you understood the day's lesson clearly. If you cannot complete the one sentence summary, ask yourself why you're stuck. Write down one or two questions you have about the topic so that you can clarify with colleagues and your professor immediately.

✓ By doing this daily work, you will eliminate the need at finals time to go back over three months' worth of notes, trying, for the first time to make sense of the material.

It is imperative that you review your notes the same day as class, while the material is fresh in your mind. This will help you focus when you organize your notes, and help you prepare for outlining later.

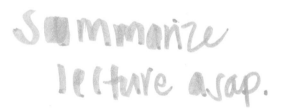

Summarize
lecture asap.

Chapter 5

Putting It Together, Part One: Synthesis

How do you put together a picnic table or a tent for camping? Do you read the directions first or ask someone for help? Do you spread out all the pieces on the floor and dare to put them together one by one?

Law school is for brave souls who love the challenge of solving a puzzle or assembling many components into one complete piece. In class, students spend hours, and in some instances days, analyzing a particular case. In the end, students are tested on how well they put together the entire puzzle on their own. Thus, rather than being tested on any particular part of the table or tent, students are tested on their assembly skills—their ability to put parts together. Whether the complete product is a table, tent or an answer to a problem of law, the same assembly skills are crucial.

This sounds good; after all, lawyers should be able to solve real life problems of real life clients; however, some law students lose sight of this goal and focus completely on the individual pieces of the puzzle. By the time the final exam comes, they may know every detail about every case they've studied in a particular course, but they have not spent even one minute putting together all the cases into one comprehensive picture. The process of taking all the individual pieces (e.g., rules from cases) and connecting them is called **synthesis**. It is the most vital skill to master to do well on exams and become a successful lawyer.

The tent you are using on your world travels needs to be assembled. How do you learn or teach yourself how to assemble it? Much like your travels, your law school journey requires you learn the skills of assembly.

Synthesis in College

In understanding the concept of synthesis in law school, it is important to identify the skills that made you successful in connecting information in your undergraduate experience. Synthesis in college usually began with the deductive method. Professors presented the big picture and then introduced more specific examples. For example, in a political science class, the professor may have presented the concept of democracy. The professor probably broke down the broad concept of democracy into smaller areas of study. He probably then discussed each small area and, in the end, put together the small and large concepts into one cohesive whole. Students then reread class notes and reading assignments and memorized key elements and concepts presented. With this method, the material was already synthesized. The professor presented both the general and the specific information students needed to know for the exam.

In other words, the professor gave you the directions for putting together a tent. The professor not only gave you the directions, but, often, she went over the directions with you in class. Perhaps you even had a chance to try out your understanding of the directions on quizzes and tests or in group projects. And if you followed the directions, you probably did very well on your exams, on which you were asked to repeat the directions and put together the same tent.

Synthesis in Law School

Unlike your undergraduate coursework, law school concepts are taught in a different manner. Instead of presenting a set of directions that are discussed and examined, law professors follow a different process:

1) Students study, in depth, various types of tents, discussing their color, shape, size, and function;

2) Students do not discuss common elements all tents share, nor do students have an opportunity to practice putting a tent together;

3) Students are not given directions on how to put a tent together;

4) Students are given several pieces of something. They are not told whether this something is a tent, sleeping bag, a lamp, or something completely different. They are then told to put the pieces together, which they must do in a very limited amount of time. They may not seek assistance from anyone during the assembly process.

To translate to law school terms, first, in a law school class, the professor presents examples of a particular concept, like battery. The reading includes cases that involve any intentional, offensive touching of one person to another. In class, specific parts of the case are examined for elements that make up this tort, but a "big picture" is not presented or even discussed in class. The law student is later supposed to "find" or "create" that big picture (that is, all of the rules and elements in a particular subject area) for him or herself using what he or she knows from individual cases. Often, students spend the first several weeks or months waiting for the professor to say, "Okay, today we are going to discuss battery and its elements. Many acts constitute a battery, including...." Instead, they read dozens of cases dealing with individual details, and, on the final exam, must apply the knowledge they have "synthesized" to a new and complex situation. In other words, you are asked to put together something for which you have never been given directions, and you don't even know what exactly it is.

Why Hide the Directions?

Many of you are probably asking, "Why would someone do this?" The answer lies within the practice of law itself. Practicing law involves many new and complex situations. Attorneys read many cases that involve similar issues and assemble all of those rules in a way that helps solve the problem at hand. The bad news is that in law school (and in law practice), you must make up your own directions, because no one will hand them over. The good news is that this process of putting together the directions can be learned. The rest of this chapter teaches you to put the pieces together so you don't have to be afraid of the phrase "some assembly required." Law school is teaching you new ways of thinking that you will employ for the rest of your professional career.

What Is Synthesis?

Synthesis is the act of putting together or connecting parts or elements to create a whole. In synthesizing cases, one combines all the rules learned from the cases to devise one rule or set of rules that encompasses a body of law. Think of this as similar to putting together a puzzle. In law school, each case teaches a rule or two. Each rule will serve as a piece of the puzzle. The professor leaves it to the student to "put together the puzzle" or figure out how all the rules fit together to create a body of law. This is the process of synthesis.

There is no one way to synthesize cases. Some cases may be easier to synthesize because each may represent a different part of the puzzle or a different element of the rule. Other cases may be more difficult to synthesize because in each, the court may seem to apply the same element in a different and confusing way. Other cases may be very difficult to synthesize because the court does not explicitly state the rule but seems to apply the same rule to a very different fact pattern; in this situation, it is ultimately the student's task to figure out the rule that the court has applied.

Tips on Synthesis

How do you compile your own set of directions for something to which you don't even have answers? Before beginning the daunting task of synthesizing rules, you inevitably must take apart each case. Thus, prior to writing an instruction manual on "how to solve tort problems," you need to deconstruct all the tort cases covered in class. Here's how to do it:

Step 1—*Gather all of the cases you have read on a particular issue.*

First, gather all the cases you have read on a particular issue or element. We will use Torts as an example. In Torts, gather all of the cases you covered on battery in intentional torts, or all of the cases you covered on negligence. If you need help figuring out which cases relate to a particular issue (for example, which cases are battery cases and which are negligence cases), consult the table of contents in your casebook and your class syllabus. In most casebooks, the editors have grouped the cases together. For example, you might find that table of contents includes the following section:

I.   Intentional Torts

   A.   Battery

      1.   The concept of intent

         a.   *Vosburg*

         b.   *Garratt*

Based on this excerpt, you know you have to synthesize *Vosburg* and *Garratt* together because they both deal with the same concept—intent.

Step 2—*Divide the cases into elements—does each case seem to represent a different element of the rule?*

The next step in synthesizing is to divide the cases into categories. To determine what the categories are, look at the definition of the issue you are tackling, and sort the cases by element. For example, in Torts, you will cover several cases on battery. Divide them into three categories based on the elements of battery: 1—intent; 2—harmful or offensive contact; and 3—with the person of another. **This is a crucial step.**

Let's return to our tent illustration. Directions for assembling a tent would lead you through a series of steps (e.g., first, put stakes in the ground, then assemble the frame, etc.). Law focuses on steps, or components, much like directions for assembling a tent. You **must not**, therefore, put things into a broad category—battery, any more than you would try to put the tent together, all parts at the same time. Instead, focus on the step, or element. Ask yourself: "Within battery, is this case about intent, harmful or offensive contact, or person?" In reality, any case can and often does touch on all of the elements of a particular issue, but cases in casebooks are heavily edited. Most cases are edited so that they illustrate only one particular element. Therefore, you should focus only on the particular element that the case is meant to teach you. **DO NOT TRY TO SYNTHESIZE CASES DEALING WITH DIFFERENT ELEMENTS!** If one case illustrates an offer, and another acceptance, the two cases obviously are not illustrating one concept.

You can synthesize cases that only deal with the same topic and element. If two cases deal with different elements of the same topic, stop there! To further our tent illustration, what we are doing at this point is isolating components of our tent—we are separating the pieces of the frame from the cover. If we return to our puzzle illustration, we are separating the blue pieces that will make up the sky from the green ones that will form the grass.

Step 3—*If, and only if, two or more cases illustrate the same element, you should divide the cases by result.*

You may read more than one case dealing with a single element. In Torts, for example, you may read more than one case dealing with the element of intent in the tort of battery. When this happens, sort the cases further by result. If you had three cases on intent in battery, you could separate those cases in which the court found intent (the "yes" cases) from those in which the court did not find intent (the "no" cases).

Now study the **similarities** between the cases within each element. What is the same among the "yes" cases? What is the same among the "no" cases?

Study the **differences** between the cases in the "yes" category and the cases in the "no" category. What separates them? Why did the court not find the element in the "no" cases, while it did find it in the "yes" cases?

> **TIP: RECAP** Remember the three steps of synthesis:
>
> 1) Gather all of the cases you have read on a particular issue.
>
> 2) Divide the cases into elements: does each case seem to represent a different element of the rule?
>
> 3) If, and only if, two or more cases illustrate the same element, you should divide the cases by result.

Formulate the **rule** for all the cases. After figuring out the similarities and the differences, you should see some sort of pattern among all the cases. The pattern you see will be the rule.

We hope that this general introduction has given you a sense of what law professors mean by "synthesis." The examples that follow will strengthen your understanding of what synthesis means and how it works. Go over each of the examples, and then try the exercises. This practice will guide you in conquering the "some assembly required" blues.

Example 1—Simple Synthesis—Torts

Each case represents a different element of the rule:

Vosburg v. Putney[1]—The court held that defendant committed a battery when defendant kicked a classmate during school and the classmate sustained serious injuries. The court found that the intent element of battery was satisfied because defendant intended to do the act (of kicking) and the act was unlawful (kicking in the classroom is prohibited, regardless of whether plaintiff intended to actually cause harm or not).

Fisher v. Carrousel Motor Hotel[2]—The court held that defendant hotel employee committed a battery when defendant willfully snatched a plate out of plaintiff conference attendee's hands and shouted that "a Negro cannot be served in the

club." The court found that although plaintiff was not actually touched (and thus not physically harmed), he was highly embarrassed and humiliated. This act constituted an offensive contact, sufficient for the harmful or offensive element of battery, because there was an offense to plaintiff's dignity with the snatching of the plate, regardless of the fact that there was no actual physical harm.

Rule/element: battery/intent and harmful or offensive contact

Result: both intent and harmful or offensive contact are essential in order to prove battery.

Because each case illustrates a separate element of battery, the two cannot be synthesized. Instead, all we can say so far in our instruction manual for battery is: *in order to be held liable for battery, the defendant must have had an intent to cause a harmful or offensive contact with the person of another, **and** a harmful or offensive contact must have occurred.* So far, that's all we know.

Example 2 — Difficult Synthesis — Torts

Each case represents the same element, but in a different way.

> *Vosburg v. Putney*[3] — The court held that the defendant committed a battery when defendant kicked a classmate during school and the classmate sustained serious injuries. The court found that the intent element of battery was satisfied because defendant intended to do the act (of kicking) and the act was unlawful (kicking in the classroom is prohibited, regardless of whether plaintiff actually intended to cause harm or not).

> *Garratt v. Dailey*[4] — The court held that the defendant committed a battery when he removed a chair from where plaintiff was attempting to sit down. The court found that the intent element of battery was satisfied because defendant knew with substantial certainty that a harmful or offensive contact would occur when defendant did the act (e.g., removed the chair).

Rule/element — battery/intent

YES	NO
Vosburg — intent to do act, and act must be unlawful	
Garratt — substantial certainty of result of actions = intent	

Similarities about cases — both focus on the intent element of battery; however, each defines intent differently.

Result: There are two different ways to prove intent; although both are not necessary, you must have one or the other.

Rule: *In order to prove intent for battery, one must prove **either** (1) defendant intended to do the act and the act was unlawful, **or** (2) defendant did the act and knew with substantial certainty that a harmful or offensive contact would result.*

Notice how our directions for making a battery have grown from the first example to the second. In example one, we were able to synthesize the big picture: to have battery, you need both intent and harmful and offensive contact. Now, we are zooming in on one particular element: intent. We are adding depth and meaning to that element. Instead of simply saying, "in putting together a tent, you will need to assemble both the frame and the cover," we are now adding; "in assembling the frame, you can use either a mallet or a hammer." In other words, we are zeroing in on a particular aspect of the project.

Example 3 — Very Difficult Synthesis — Property[5]

Each case seems to represent the same rule and the same element, but the court has not explicitly stated the rule.

> *May v. Rice* — The court held that Tenant A could assert constructive eviction as a defense to an action for rent due by his landlord. The tenant was displaced when the pizza parlor located below his apartment burst into flames and all of his clothing and other furnishings were ruined by smoke damage.
>
> *Strong v. Strange* — The court held that Tenant B could successfully defend an action by his landlord for rent due, when he was constructively evicted in the dead of winter when the apartment's boiler blew up and the apartment's temperature plunged with the sub-zero weather outside.
>
> *Cramdon v. Carney* — The court held that Tenant C could not successfully assert a constructive eviction defense against an action for unpaid rent when she moved out because her neighbors were rowdy, threw wild parties, and generally made far too much noise.

Rule/element — constructive eviction ... (notice that there are no separate elements for us to consider; hence we divide the cases by result)

YES	NO
May — apartment burst into flames; everything in apartment ruined by smoke	*Cramdon* — rowdy, loud neighbors, too much noise
Strange — boiler blew up, temperature in apartment plunged, sub-zero outside	

Similarities/Differences: "Yes" cases — both smoke damage and low temperatures create a health hazard or a safety issue (impossible to live in either environment). Rowdy neighbors do not create health or safety hazard (one can live with noise, even though it is bothersome).

Result: Safety and/or health hazard is key for constructive eviction.

Rule: *In order to assert constructive eviction as a defense for an action for unpaid rent, the tenant must be able to prove that a safety issue or health hazard prevented him or her from living in the apartment. A mere nuisance, such as noise, that does not endanger health or safety, is insufficient.*

Notice how far we've come from Example One to Example Three. Here, we really have to think in putting together an instruction manual for constructive eviction. The court does not set forth elements for us to consider. When there are no elements, we have to go right to the comparison step. Again, however frightening it may be to do so, because there is no way to check your answer, *it is crucial to engage in this type of thinking.* How can you know that your conclusion (that the crucial factor is health and safety) is correct? This is a difficult question to answer. Indeed, some law students and lawyers may come to a different conclusion as to what the key point is distinguishing the "yes" cases from the "no" cases; however, keep one important point in mind: **AS LONG AS THE CONCLUSION CAN BE SUPPORTED BY THE CASES, IT IS A LEGITIMATE POINT.** If one or more of the cases do not fit your model, then you must adjust it. If, **all** cases can be put into the model, your model is sound, even if someone else has a different one to explain the difference in result.

Synthesis Exercises

Exercise 5-1
Synthesis: Statutory Interpretation

Ekl v. Knecht[6] — A plumber arrived at the Ekl home to repair a leaky pipe. After finishing the work, the plumber presented Mrs. Ekl with a bill for an exorbitant amount. When Mrs. Ekl protested, the plumber refused to leave her home and threatened to undo the work if she did not pay. Mrs. Ekl sued the plumber, claiming that he violated the state's Deceptive Trade and Business Practices Act. The court agreed. In order to violate the statute, a defendant must have committed either an unfair or deceptive act. Here, the plumber's actions were clearly unfair because it is both immoral and illegal to threaten someone's person or property in order to secure payment for services.

Crowder v. Oberling[7] — The defendant, a used car salesperson, violated the Deceptive Trade and Business Practices Act when he represented a car to a customer as a "good used car." The customer later discovered that the car had been involved in numerous accidents and was a salvaged vehicle. The court found that the defendant engaged in deceptive conduct under the Act because he misrepresented that the car was "good" when he knew it had an extensive history of safety problems. This knowledge stemmed from his extensive experience in the car business and his knowledge that the cars he was purchasing at auction were at a far lower price than others that were considered "good cars."

Answer to Exercise 5-1
Synthesis: Statutory Construction

Rule/element: Deceptive Trade and Business Practices Act/unfair or deceptive acts.

Result: One must prove that another's conduct was either deceptive or unfair in order to establish liability under the Act.

NOTE: Because each case illustrates a separate aspect of the Act, the cases cannot be synthesized together. Instead, all we can say so far is that you need either an unfair or deceptive act to establish liability. If we could elaborate, it would only be to say that unfair acts seem to be those that involve threats to a person or property, and deceptive ones involve a misrepresentation of fact, which the defendant knows to be false.

Exercise 5-2
Synthesis: Criminal Law

Case #1 — In order for school officials to search a student's personal belongings, the search must comport with the Fourth Amendment. In other words, the authority must have probable cause to search. In cases involving minors in schools, the probable cause standard is met when school officials can prove that they had a reasonable suspicion that the student was involved in illegal activity. Here, the student in question had a reputation for drug use, had been previously caught with drugs, and had bragged to others in the hall that she "did a line" during lunch breaks. The school officials had a reasonable suspicion to search the student, given her familiarity with drugs.

Case #2 — A student claimed that the principal's search of his backpack violated his Fourth Amendment rights. The student had not been involved with drugs, nor had he been seen using or selling drugs on a previous occasion. The student did associate with known drug users and was standing on a street corner, just outside school grounds, that was known for drug activity, when the principal, on his way to work, asked to see his backpack. The principal searched the backpack and discovered a small amount of marijuana. The principal claimed that he had probable cause to search. The principal argued that the student's association with known drug users and his presence in an area known for drug activity formed the basis of the principal's "reasonable suspicion." His argument was meritorious. Although his suspicion was not based on the individual's past, given the other circumstantial evidence, it was "reasonable."

Answer to Exercise 5-2
Synthesis: Criminal Law

Rule/element: Fourth Amendment — probable cause — reasonable suspicion (notice that it is important to break this down in this order because the court does so). The only question that remains is what constitutes "reasonable" suspicion?

YES   NO

Case #1

Suspicion is reasonable based on the
individual's past. Factors such as the
individual's familiarity with drugs,
past drug use, and prior charges can
all establish reasonable suspicion.

Case #2

Suspicion is reasonable even though
individual himself might not be familiar
with drugs or have prior charges but does
associate with known drug users and is
found on property known for its drug trade.

Similarities in the cases: Both cases focus on what "reasonable" suspicion means for purposes of searching a student's property, yet they each define reasonable suspicion differently. The first case uses a more stringent standard (i.e., there must be knowledge of the individual's drug familiarity before searching), while the second case seems to relax the standard somewhat to include outside factors (i.e., an individual's friends and his location at the time of search).

Rule: The reasonable suspicion standard may be met one of two ways.

Result: To prove that the search of a student's property was based on a reasonable suspicion, school officials need to show either: (1) knowledge of the individual student's familiarity with drugs, or (2) knowledge that the individual's friends are familiar with drugs or that the location at the time of search is known for drug activity.

Exercise 5-3
Synthesis: Contracts

America v. Henson—Mr. Henson claims a portion of his employment contract should not be enforced because it is unconscionable. His employer argues that: (1) Henson had a clear choice as to whether to accept employment under the terms and conditions offered; and (2) Henson read the contract and signed it without any questions whatsoever. The court concluded that understanding the terms of the contract or the choices presented is not the test for unconscionability. The test is overreaching by a contracting party in an unfairly superior bargaining position. We think the test here has been met in view of the fact that Henson had not only begun his employment but had relocated before receiving and reviewing the written contract.

Heller v. Convalescent Home[8]—Courts will readily find contracts unconscionable between consumers and skilled corporate sellers; however, courts are reluctant to rewrite terms of a negotiated contract between businesspeople. Still, the overarching inquiry is whether a party was in an unfair bargaining position with the other. In this case, the contract providing for a lease of computers to a convalescent home was not unconscionable when: (1) although certain provisions of the lease favored one party, all provisions were agreed to by parties of equal bargaining strength; and (2) the lease price was not excessive for the product.

Bunge Co. v. Williams[9] — The fact that the disclaimer of warranties was not specifically pointed out to the consumer by the seller did not render the contract unenforceable against the buyer, at least when the front of the contract stated, in bold letters: "ALL WARRANTIES, EXPRESS AND IMPLIED, ARE DISCLAIMED."

DON'T WORRY: This problem involves a very difficult synthesis. If you did not get this far in your synthesis right away, don't worry. You may be able to "solve" it in time. Return to this task later in the semester. Synthesis is a crucial skill that ought not be ignored; however, it is a skill that develops over time. Be patient.

Answer to Exercise 5-3
Synthesis: Contracts

Rule/element: Unconscionable contracts. Because neither court expressly stated any elements, we must engage in a complex synthesis. Putting the cases on the yes/no grid, we can come up with:

YES	NO
Henson: Test for unconscionability is overreaching by a contracting party in an unfairly superior bargaining position.	*Heller*: Court looked at (1) bargaining strength of parties and (2) price (not excessive) to determine whether contract was unconscionable when parties were both business people.
When one party has not had the opportunity to read and review a contract before acting on it, it is very likely that the contract is unconscionable, especially when the contract is between a consumer and a businessperson.	*Bunge*: Court found contract enforceable (not unconscionable) between a consumer and a businessperson when a disclaimer was on front of contract and in big bold letters.

Similarities/Differences: *Henson* says that the test for unconscionablity is unfair bargaining position between the parties. In *Henson*, the test was met because plaintiff (a consumer) did not have a chance to read and review the contract before acting upon it. Note that this case involved a consumer and businessperson. In another case involving a consumer, the court found that the business did not engage in unconscionable behavior by failing to point out a disclaimer to the consumer. The court found it important that the consumer had the contract before making a decision and the disclaimer was on the front page of the document, set off in bold print. Finally, although the *Heller* case involved two business people, the court nonetheless subscribed to the main rule: the test for unconscionability is an unfair bargaining position. The *Heller* court broke down the concept of an unfair bargaining position into more specific criteria: (1) bargaining strength of the parties and (2) excessive price.

Result: To prove a contract unconscionable, one must show that the parties are in an unfair bargaining position.

Rule: When a court evaluates unconscionability, the key factor is the degree of overreaching by a contracting party in an unfairly superior bargaining position. This test is most likely *not* satisfied if the parties have equal bargaining power, such as two businesses. To more specifically assess whether one party is in an unfairly superior bargaining position, courts consider both the terms of the contract and the excessiveness of the price. A court also may find a contract unconscionable if a disclaimer of liability is hidden in the contract, rather than clearly displayed on the front of the contract in big bold letters.

Endnotes

1. This information is based on *Vosburg v. Putney*, 56 N.W. 480 (Wis. 1893).

2. This information is based on *Fisher v. Carrousel Motor Hotel, Inc.*, 424 S.W.2d 627(Tex. 1967).

3. This information is based on *Vosburg v. Putney*, 56 N.W. 480 (Wis. 1893).

4. This information is based on *Garratt v. Dailey*, 49 Wash. 2d 499 (1956).

5. © 1993 Cathaleen A. Roach, used with permission.

6. This information is based on *Ekl v. Knecht*, 585 N.E.2d 156 (Ill. App. Ct. 1991).

7. This information is based on *Crowder v. Bob Oberling Enter.*, 499 N.E.2d 115 (Ill. App. Ct. 1986).

8. This information is based on *Heller v. Convalescent Home*, 365 N.E.2d 1285 (Ill. App. Ct. 1977).

9. This information is based on *Bunge Co. v. Williams*, 359 N.E.2d 844 (Ill. App. Ct. 1977).

Chapter 6

Putting It Together, Part Two: The Role of the Law School Outline

Have you ever bought a travel guide for a vacation and found that it would serve you better with additional or even different information? Or, after searching through several different guides, have you ever found that combining parts from one with those of another created the perfect companion to your trip? Have you ever seen a travel guide without a map? Finding the right travel guide is like finding the right outline for a law school class. The best travel guides provide background information on the area, list the best sites to see and when to see them, warn of potential pratfalls, and suggest the best ways out of troublesome situations. Likewise, an outline serves the same purpose for law school finals. A well-prepared outline can provide directions for answering complicated law school exam questions, including guidance on likely questions, specific issues to look for, and the best approaches and solutions.

You may have heard that outlines are the key to success in law school. Law students and professors agree: prepare a good outline and you'll get a good grade. First year students often think that picking up a commercial outline at the bookstore or copying one from a second or third year student will prepare them for exams; however, merely acquiring a "good" outline will not suffice. Instead, you need to understand, organize, and synthesize the material you cover over a semester so that you can apply it to different fact situations. To do this, you must take an active approach to "learning the law." The best way to accomplish this goal is to make your own outline. Indeed, the process of preparing an outline or a flowchart[1] itself helps students "learn the law," resulting in better exam performance.[2] With that idea in mind, this chapter explains what a law school outline is, describes different kinds of outlines, and provides techniques for making useful, concise outlines.

What Is an Outline?

An outline is a compilation of definitions, rules, case blurbs, and other important information that functions as a student's private tour guide for the class. A good outline achieves three ends. First, it helps you learn the law and how the law is applied. A good outline uses examples from both actual cases and hypothetical fact patterns to illustrate points of law. Second, it provides ammunition for answering specific exam questions. Third, it helps you memorize rules, which is particularly crucial for closed book exams.

What Are the Different Kinds of Outlines?

Outlines are of two types: commercial (*i.e.*, store-bought) and homemade (*i.e.*, student-prepared). Commercial outlines are researched by publishers and sold in law school bookstores all over the country. They are written in an encyclopedia-like format and include mainly general and some specific information. Commercial outlines generally define the rules of law and often include cases or hypothetical fact patterns as examples. Some commercial outlines also include essay and multiple choice questions with answers. Commercial outlines have some advantages: they can be helpful by illustrating legal concepts and providing memory devices, they are easy to obtain, and they require no preparation.

Homemade outlines, on the other hand, are made by students from their own materials. Obviously, a student's own outline will be personalized, written in his own terminology and tailored to a specific class taught by a specific professor. Homemade outlines require additional work beyond class preparation. Like commercial outlines, student-prepared outlines include definitions and rules of law, along with cases and hypotheticals. They also contain specific information from class notes on the professor's ideas about the law and individual cases. Student-prepared outlines are similar to commercial outlines in some respects, but a homemade outline tends to prepare students for an exam better than a commercial outline can. Why? A fundamental truth of law school is that exams are "professor-specific." That is, a professor is more likely to award a higher grade to an answer that addresses an issue in the same way as he or she did in class. The best way to "see" an issue the professor's way is to prepare your own outline from your own notes on what your professor covered. Remember no matter how good a travel guide is, nothing can capture your experiences more accurately than your **own** travel journal.

Going over class notes and synthesizing daily can lead to a well-made personalized outline. This may sound stressful and time-consuming, especially when there is reading to do for the next day. However, going over your notes and organizing your thoughts will help you remember and continue to be organized in the future. In creating your own outline, you prompt yourself to remember the class and specific theories that the professor was stressing, and the hypothetical proposed. If you work this way during the semester, you can save valuable time at the end of the year. Having an outline that you created will also be incredibly helpful if your professor allows you to bring in notes to the final, as it is a much better reference tool if created to your own style of learning and thinking. Using a commercial outline might seem like an excellent idea, but often they include information your class was not required to learn, and you can become confused on non-relevant issues. That is not to say that commercial outlines are not useful; combining ideas and information from one with your own personalized version can be incredibly helpful for your comprehension and reference later.

What Kind of Outline Should I Use — Commercial or Homemade?

Remember the travel guide that included everything except a map? A commercial outline is like such a travel guide: it gives useful *general* information about an area but does not tell you exactly how to get to a *specific* place. Given such a shortcoming, a homemade outline serves you well because it includes professor- and class-specific information. Despite this, some students may think, "Why should I reinvent the wheel? If someone has already prepared an outline, why do I have to do it again?" Do not fall into this trap. The number one benefit of creating your own outline is that the process of reviewing your briefs and class notes to prepare the outline will force you to "learn the law." Some claim that once you've done an outline, you can throw it away. Extreme perhaps, but the basic premise is true. The real value of an outline is in *making* it, not *having* it. The work you do in preparing your own outline facilitates learning not just the law, but how to apply it. The exercise of creating an outline prepares you for finals better than merely studying someone else's, because the information becomes "owned," rather than "borrowed."

Another reason for preparing your own outline, as opposed to purchasing one or borrowing one, is that your own outline will be class- and professor-specific. That is, it will correspond directly to all the cases you read and discussed in class. It will include specific information from your class notes and from your professor. This will be much more helpful than a commercial outline, which might include more information than you covered in class (and actually may confuse you) or might not include the most recent or even the same cases you read for class. Your professor could want specific cases that your class studied in depth, and the hypothetical that you specifically learned. A commercial outline will not provide it, nor will outlines passed on through classes. Perhaps you say, "If that's the case, then I can just borrow or copy an outline from a second or third year student who already took this class with the same professor." An outline from another student may be more helpful than a commercial outline, but you must consider a few important factors when borrowing outlines from other students. You need to know how well that student did in the class. You certainly don't want an outline from a C student. Whether or not that student had the same professor, you need to know whether the professor is using the same book and whether the law has changed. Taking all these factors into account, you still may find an outline that seems suitable for your class; however, this will never take the place of creating your own. By not going through the process of organizing the material, you are not learning how the rules relate to various facts, because you do not see them in practice. Thus, you are missing the big picture: you are not "learning the law," and you are not learning how to apply it. Instead, you are reading and memorizing information, which will not help you answer your exam questions. To return to our travel analogy, it is the difference between reading about a country and visiting it yourself.

TIP: In sum, you should make your own outline because:

✓ The process of making it will force you to learn the law;

✓ Your outline will be specific to a class and professor;

✓ Making your own outline requires you to synthesize and apply the law, which you will be required to do on the exam.

What Should a Good Outline Include?

The following is a summary of the information you should include in your outline. However, keep in mind that this is a sample of just **one** way to organize your outline and not the **only** way. (See the sample outlines at the end of this chapter).

I. Main topic or issue

   A. What are the main policies in this area of law?

   B. What are the rules? Include definition and elements, if any.

      1. Case examples of when rule has and has not been violated.

      2. Hypos from class as examples of how the rule is applied.

   C. When will I see this on an exam? What should I look for?

   D. More policy (if applicable)—make sure you focus on what your professor brings up in class.

      1. Do these rules serve the policies of this area of law?

      2. Is this a good rule or a bad rule? (Will the rule help or hurt society?)

II. Main topic or issue

How to Make Your Own Outline

Congratulations if you have decided to make your own outlines! It will be a daunting task, but one you can accomplish if you follow the steps and techniques provided below.

In reading individual cases and preparing for class, you focused on specific information. You discussed individual rules and elements of those rules and how courts applied them in different cases. In your outline, you need to focus on the general information or the big picture. Your task is to determine how the many different rules fit together and interact as a whole. The first step in this process is called synthesis. (For more information on synthesis, see Chapter 4.) You should begin synthesizing the rules every other week as you begin to review the material. The second step is outlining. In order

outline template

to begin outlining, you need to set aside a large block of time, approximately three to five hours, and have the following materials available:

3-5 hr per outline

- Casebook
- Syllabus
- Case briefs
- Class notes
- Hornbook and/or commercial outline*

* Optional items, as some students are able to create their own outline without the use of a hornbook or commercial outline. On the other hand, many students find both to be helpful in grasping the material.

Step 1 — Get the big picture.

Refer to your course syllabus and the table of contents in your casebook to get a feel for the big picture. Examine how the material is organized. What are the major headings, and what are the sub-headings below them? Depending on how your syllabus or table of contents is organized, you may benefit from a hornbook or commercial outline as another source in determining which issues are big issues and which are sub-issues. Use this information as a template or skeleton for your own outline. Begin with the syllabus or table of contents, and fill in the blanks with buzzwords, definitions, and case names. See the example below based on the course syllabus in Chapter 2.

Sample Outline #1 — Torts

Intentional Torts

    Battery

        Intent

            Vosburg v. Putney

            Garratt v. Dailey

        Harmful or Offensive Contact

    Negligence

    Strict Liability

Step 2 — Insert the rules.

After you have created a skeleton, the next step is to insert the rules into your outline. Before listing all the rules, however, you should synthesize them. (See Chapter 4.) Once you have synthesized the rules, add all of them to your outline; break them down into elements, if necessary. This may involve stating a general rule or definition and then listing all the elements and exceptions. See sample below.

Sample Outline #2 — Torts

Intentional Torts

    I.   Battery

        A. The intentional causing of harmful or offensive contact with the person of another.

            1. Intent

                a. Subjective — The defendant actually wanted to cause harmful or offensive contact with the person of another.

                b. Objective — The defendant committed an act that a reasonably prudent person with ordinary sensibilities would have foreseen would cause harmful or offensive contact with the person of another.

            2. Harmful or Offensive Contact

                a. Defendant is liable for contacts that cause actual physical harm AND

                b. For contacts that are insulting. A plaintiff is entitled to demand that the defendant refrain from the offensive touching, though the contact results in no visible injury.

            3. Person — The defendant is liable for contact with the plaintiff's person.

Step 3 — Insert cases and hypotheticals.

    Now that your outline contains rules and elements, your next step is to understand how each rule and element is applied. Return to the individual cases and hypotheticals discussed in class. What point does each case or hypothetical illustrate? You must determine the rule and/or element that each represents and include a "blurb," or very brief summary, to explain how that rule or element is applied. Include a sentence or two on the relevant facts to aid in your explanation. Be sure to note what kinds of facts trigger each issue or element of the rule. See example below.

Sample Outline #3 — Torts

Intentional Torts

    I.   Battery

        A. The intentional causing of harmful or offensive contact with the person of another

            1. Intent

                a. Subjective — The defendant actually wanted to cause harmful or offensive contact with the person of another.

                    1) Court found intent

                        Vosburg v. Putney:

D kicked P in shin after class was called to order. Court said D intended to kick him (even though D did not intend severe injury), so we have intent to satisfy this element of battery.

    b.   Objective — The defendant committed an act that a reasonably prudent person with ordinary sensibilities would have foreseen would cause harmful or offensive contact with the person of another.

        1) *Garratt v. Dailey:* No intent, but knew with substantial certainty injury would occur

Defendant pulled a chair from underneath an elderly lady while she was about to sit in the chair. As a result of the chair being swiped from underneath her, the lady fell and broke her hip. Although the defendant did not intend for the lady to break her hip, a reasonably prudent person with ordinary sensibilities could have foreseen with substantial certainty that the lady would be injured (pulling a chair usually leads to a fall, which, in turn leads to an injury); therefore, the defendant intended to cause the lady's injuries.

  2.   Harmful or Offensive Contact

    a.   Defendant is liable for contacts that cause actual physical harm AND

    b.   For contacts that are insulting. A plaintiff is entitled to demand that the defendant refrain from the offensive touching, though the contact results in no visible injury.

Offensive contact (defined by religion)

Hypo: A male nurse aids in the operation of a woman whose religion prohibits her from being touched by a male. The operation was successful. The nurse is liable for battery because he caused an insulting and offensive contact to the woman, even though no visible injury resulted.

  3.   Person — The defendant is liable for contact with the plaintiff's person.

Offensive contact (touched "extension" of person)

Hypo: The defendant publicly insulted plaintiff and grabbed a plate from the plaintiff's hand. Although the defendant did not actually touch the plaintiff, he committed a battery because he forged offensive contact with an extension of the plaintiff's person (*i.e.*, the plate he held in his hand).

Note that the cases illustrate elements of rules. The most common mistake students make is using cases as the focus of the outline. In other words, the outline is nothing more than a series of case summaries. Remember, in and of themselves cases are irrelevant, they are only important in so far as they illustrate how an element of the rule works.

make my focus!

Step 4—Insert the reasons/rationale for the rules (policy).

Now that your outline contains rules, elements of the rules, and cases and hypotheticals showing how to apply the rules, you should be able to use this information to make solid arguments either for or against the rule, based on the elements or cases. In addition to these arguments, you may need to argue policy. Policy arguments include analysis of whether a law or a particular application of the law is fair or just in terms of several factors. These factors include the history of the law, whom the law was intended to protect, and the impact of the law on society (*i.e.*, whether it benefits society or causes more problems). Arguing policy may involve a discussion of social, economic, political, and governmental concerns. Information will come primarily from your notes on class discussion. If your professor lectured on how a particular case changed the law (for example, by creating requirements for forming contracts), then you need to include that information in your outline. You may be able to use the reason behind the rule or the policy implications of the rule to argue for or against the application of a rule. See sample outline below.

Sample Outline #4—Torts

Intentional Torts

    I.   Battery

        A. The intentional causing of harmful or offensive contact with the person of another

            1.   Intent

                a.   Subjective—The defendant actually wanted to cause harmful or offensive contact with the person of another.

                     1) Court found intent

                         Vosburg v. Putney:

                         D kicked P in shin after class was called to order. Court said D intended to kick him (even though D did not intend severe injury), so we have intent to satisfy this element of battery.

                b.   Objective—The defendant committed an act that a reasonably prudent person with ordinary sensibilities would have foreseen would cause harmful or offensive contact with the person of another.

                     1) *Garratt v. Dailey:* No intent, but knew with substantial certainty injury would occur

                         Defendant pulled a chair from underneath an elderly lady while she was about to sit in the chair. As a result of the chair being swiped from underneath her, the lady fell and broke her hip. Although the defendant did not intend for the lady to break her hip, a reasonably prudent person with ordinary sensibilities could have foreseen with substantial certainty that the lady would be injured (pulling a chair usually leads to a fall, which, in turn leads to an injury); therefore, the defendant intended to cause the lady's injuries.

2. Harmful or Offensive Contact

    a. Defendant is liable for contacts that cause actual physical harm AND

    b. For contacts that are insulting. A plaintiff is entitled to demand that the defendant refrain from the offensive touching, though the contact results in no visible injury.

    Offensive contact (defined by religion)

    Hypo: A male nurse aids in the operation of a woman whose religion prohibits her from being touched by a male. The operation was successful. The nurse is liable for battery because he caused an insulting and offensive contact to the woman, even though no visible injury resulted.

3. Person—The defendant is liable for contact with the plaintiff's person.

    Offensive contact (touched "extension" of person)

    Hypo: The defendant publicly insulted plaintiff and grabbed a plate from the plaintiff's hand. Although the defendant did not actually touch the plaintiff, he committed a battery because he forged offensive contact with an extension of the plaintiff's person (*i.e.*, the plate he held in his hand).

    Policy: When something is so close to the victim's person that it is an extension of him (*i.e.*, an object held in his hand), a wrongdoer is liable. Battery protects individuals from hurt and offense—intentional interference with an object held in plaintiff's hand, even if not hurtful, is no less offensive.

Additional Tips on Outlining:
Open Book v. Closed Book Exams

An outline may differ substantially for an open book exam and a closed book exam. In open book exams, professors allow students to use materials, often including their casebook, other required texts, and the students' own homemade outline during the exam. Commercial outlines usually are forbidden. In closed book exams, students are not permitted to bring anything into the exam. You can imagine how your outline might be different depending on the type of exam. For an open book exam, you might seek a user-friendly, visual outline. You can make your outline user-friendly by making an index or table of contents and dividing the outline with tabs. This will allow you to easily locate a particular rule or case. You should include some type of flowchart (see Chapter 6) or an issue checklist. Having a list of all the issues covered over the year or semester will help in a couple of ways. One, it will help you stay focused on the exam because you will be focused on the issues on your checklist. Two, if you get stuck and are unsure if you are on the right track, you can refer to the checklist to make sure you have not forgotten something. (For more on using a checklist during the exam, see Chapter 9: Tips on Exam Preparation.) For a closed book exam, you need to prepare an outline that will enable you to both remember the law and to work through the steps in the analysis. For a closed book exam, you should begin with a comprehensive outline and then keep reducing it to something you can visualize (about ten to twenty pages per course). A flowchart is also a very helpful way to reduce your comprehensive outline into something more manageable.

TIP: When outlining remember to follow these four steps:

1) Refer to your syllabus or table of contents for the big picture.
2) Synthesize the rules and break them down into elements.
3) Insert the cases and hypos (as examples of how to apply the rules) into your outline.
4) Insert the reasons/rationale for the rule (policy) into your outline.

Additional Tips on Outlining: Outlining Software

Technology can help you create and manage your outline. Remember, the goal is to outline material to improve your understanding of the rules and the application. So, if you decide to use a computer program to assist you with outlining, make sure it helps your learning and does not hinder your progress.

The first program you should consider is Outliner by StoreLaw. This program is available at www.storelaw.com. It is a program specifically created for law students. Because it is created for law students, it includes a lot of features for your specific needs, such as templates created specifically for certain casebooks, and links to free case briefs online at Lexis.com and Westlaw.com.[3] Although Outliner will have access to this material, you want to be careful about "cutting and pasting" information from case briefs directly into your outline. You want to make certain that you understand the material and are not simply copying it from one location to another. Finally, Outliner also works with Microsoft Word and other word processing programs to allow you to transfer the information you put into the outline into other formats.

The second program that may assist you in outlining and getting organized is OneNote by Microsoft. This product is available at *office.microsoft.com*. OneNote is an electronic notebook or folder. It allows you to link a flowchart to a document, such as an outline or your typewritten or scanned notes. You can add graphics, photos, pictures, flashcards, spreadsheets, etc. This product can also be used for research projects and managing tasks and teams of people working with several documents.

The final program, OmniOutliner, is for Mac users. This program is good for creating outlines, as well as to-do lists and other organizational tools. You can also hide portions of the outline while you work on other portions and you can see all of the major headings by clicking one button so that you can remain focused.

Of course, this is not an exhaustive list of all of the software programs on outlining, but just a sample of those for you to consider. Remember, you must do what works best for you. So if you find that handwriting your outline on a legal pad works, do that. If you prefer to simply type out your outline into your word processing software and add the Roman numerals or numbers or letters yourself, then go for it. However, if you prefer a computer program that will help you organize the material, then you should research these and other programs to find the best fit for your needs.

Outlining Exercises

Exercise 6-1
Outlining: Contracts

Step 1—Fill in the blanks of the outline using the following concepts:

A contract is an offer, an acceptance, and a consideration. Promises that are not meant to be legally binding (illusory promises or promise of a gift) are not contracts. They are deemed to be "mere promises." Contracts are based on the principle of mutual assent to a bargain. A mutual assent to a bargain means that both parties intend to enter into a binding contractual relationship. Courts will not enforce agreements that were made in jest or that the parties themselves did not take seriously. In order to determine whether the parties had a mutual assent to a bargain, courts consider objective, rather than subjective, factors. In other words, what one of the parties thought she was entering into is not as important as what the parties said, what was exchanged, what was witnessed by others, and what was acted upon at the time. If it looks like a contract to a reasonable person, then it's a contract.

I. Parts of a contract

    A.

    B.

    C.

II. Determining whether you have a contract or a "mere promise"

    A. What to look for:

    B. How you know if you have a contract:

        1) Not present when....

        2) Does exist if:

            a)

            b)

            c)

            d)

    C. In sum, you have a contract when ...

Answer to Exercise 6-1
Step 1

I.   Parts of a contract

　　A.   Offer

　　B.   Acceptance

　　C.   Consideration

II. Determining whether you have a contract or a "mere promise"

　　A.   What to look for: mutual assent to a bargain

　　B.   How you know if you have it:

　　　　1)   Not present when all you have is a party's subjective thoughts and intentions

　　　　2)   Does exist when there are objective signs of an intent to enter into a bargain

　　　　　　a)   what did the parties say?

　　　　　　b)   what did the parties exchange?

　　　　　　c)   what did others see / hear?

　　　　　　d)   what did the parties do at the time?

　　C.   In sum, when it looks like a contract to a reasonable person, then it's a contract.

Step 2—Add the following case examples to the outline in the appropriate place:

Lucy[4]: D and P got drunk, and P asked to purchase D's farm. D agreed, thinking P was joking. The next day, D withdrew acceptance. P contended he did not have reason to believe D was joking and tendered payment; therefore, D could not withdraw. Court held that the contract was enforceable because the outward conduct of both parties indicated an intent to bargain. Specifically, the parties wrote out the terms on a napkin, sent for witnesses, and signed a note memorializing their agreement.

Bombry[5]: P approached D to renew P's employment contract. D expressed agreement to renew contract for one year. Two months later, D fired P. D contended that no contract existed because D did not really intend to enter into a contract with P. Court held that D's undisclosed intent was immaterial because a reasonable person would conclude that a bargain was made based on (1) previous renewals that were honored, (2) the circumstances surrounding the renewal (D had repeatedly assured P that "she would be around for a long time"), and (3) the business environment in which the renewal was negotiated (in D's office on a day when employee reviews were being conducted)

Dickinson[6]: D agreed to hold open the sale of property to P for two days. The next day P learned that D intended to sell the property to someone else. P raced to catch D before D left town on a train. Court held that the actions of both parties—D offering to sell to third party and P scrambling to beat the second sale—manifested both parties' belief that a contract did not exist.

Answer to Exercise 6-1
Step 2

I. Parts of a contract

    A. Offer

    B. Acceptance

    C. Consideration

II. Determining whether you have a contract or a "mere promise"

    A. What to look for: mutual assent to a bargain

    B. How you know if you have it:

        1) Not present when all you have is a party's subjective thoughts and intentions

        2) Does exist when there are objective signs of an intent to enter into a bargain

            a) what did the parties say?

            b) what did the parties exchange?

            c) what did others see / hear?

            d) what did the parties do at the time?

    C. In sum, when it looks like a contract to a reasonable person, then it's a contract.

        1) "looks like a contract to a reasonable person" (because of writing, witnesses and signatures)

            Lucy: D and P got drunk and P asked to purchase D's farm. D agreed, thinking P was joking. The next day, D withdrew acceptance. P contended he did not have reason to believe D was joking, and tendered payment; therefore, D could not withdraw. Court held that the contract was enforceable because the outward conduct of both parties indicated an intent to bargain. Specifically, the parties wrote out the terms on a napkin, sent for witnesses, and signed a note memorializing their agreement.

        2) "looks like a contract to a reasonable person" (because of assurances, location and timing of conversation)

            Bombry: P approached D to renew P's employment contract. D expressed agreement to renew contract for one year. Two months later, D fired P. D contended that no contract existed because D did not really intend to enter into a contract with P. Court held that D's undisclosed intent was immaterial because a reasonable person would conclude that a bargain was made based on (1) previous renewals that were honored, (2) the circumstances surrounding the renewal (D had repeatedly assured P that "she would be around for a long time"), and (3) the business environment in which the renewal was negotiated (in D's office on a day when employee reviews were being conducted).

        3) "does NOT look like a contract to a reasonable person" (because no terms and no specifics)

Dickinson: D agreed to hold open the sale of property to P for two days. The next day P learned that D intended to sell the property to someone else. P raced to catch D before D left town on a train. Court held that the actions of both parties—D offering to sell to third party and P scrambling to beat the second sale—manifested both parties' belief that a contract did not exist.

Exercise 6-2
Outlining: Criminal Law

Step 1—Fill in the blanks of the outline using the following concepts:

The actus reus committed with the mens rea, absent any defenses, results in criminal liability. People are blameworthy only when they act on their own free will, that is, when they make a conscious choice to act; this is the policy of punishment for criminal acts; therefore, the actus reus, or physical act, must be a voluntary act in order for the actor to be blameworthy. If an act is reflexive or unconscious, then it is not voluntary and is not committed by the actor's free will; therefore, it is not blameworthy.

The actus reus alone is insufficient for criminal liability. The culpable act must also be committed with the requisite mental state, or mens rea. The voluntary act becomes a guilty act when the actor has both the intent to bring about a result and the knowledge that the act will bring about such a result. Like the actus reus, the policy for punishment is that people are blameworthy only when they make a conscious choice to act.

There are defenses to criminal liability. One is self-defense. Another is insanity.

I.

    A.

    B.

II.

    A.

    B.

    C.

III.

    A.

    B.

Answer to Exercise 6-2
Step 1

I. Actus Reus

    A. Policy: people are blameworthy only when they act on their own free will.

    B. Act must be voluntary. An unconscious or reflexive act is NOT voluntary, and the actor is not blameworthy.

II. Mens Rea

  A. Policy: people are blameworthy only when they act on their own free will. Awareness that one's act will bring about a harmful consequence is blameworthy.

  B. Intent

  C. Knowledge

III. Defenses

  A. Self-defense

  B. Insanity

Step 2—Add the following case examples to the outline in the appropriate place:

Martin[7]: D got drunk at home. Police dragged him out into the street, then cited him for public intoxication. Court held D not culpable because he was not in public as a result of his own voluntary act.

Newton[8]: After being shot in his stomach, D shot a police officer. D then fled to a hospital for treatment. D claimed that the shot to his stomach caused a reflexive impulse to shoot back; and because he was acting from reflex, he was not conscious at the time he shot the police officer. Court held that if D's action was a reflex, it was not conscious and thus was not voluntary. Therefore, D had a complete defense.

Decina[9]: D, an epileptic, crashed his car and killed four people. D claimed that because he had a seizure while driving, crashing was not a voluntary act. Court held that because D knew he was subject to seizures, his voluntary act of getting into a car to drive was a voluntary undertaking of the risk of seizure while driving; thus, his act was voluntary.

Answer to Exercise 6-2
Step 2

I. Actus Reus

  A. Policy: people are blameworthy only when they act on their own free will.

  B. Act must be voluntary. An unconscious or reflexive act is NOT voluntary, and the actor is not blameworthy.

    1. Not voluntary—drunk

       Martin: D got drunk at home. Police dragged him out into the street, then cited him for public intoxication. Court held D not culpable because he was not in public as a result of his own voluntary act.

    2. Not voluntary—reflex

       Newton: After being shot in his stomach, D shot a police officer. D then fled to a hospital for treatment. D claimed that the shot to his stomach caused a reflexive impulse to shoot back; and because he was acting from reflex, he was not conscious at the time he shot the police officer. Court held that if D's action was a reflex, it was not conscious and thus was not voluntary. Therefore, D had a complete defense.

3. Voluntary—knew prone to seizures and voluntarily took risk

Decina: D, an epileptic, crashed his car and killed four people. D claimed that because he had a seizure while driving, crashing was not a voluntary act. Court held that because D knew he was subject to seizures, his voluntary act of getting into a car to drive was a voluntary undertaking of the risk of seizure while driving; thus, his act was voluntary.

II. Mens Rea

   A. Policy: people are blameworthy only when they act on their own free will. Awareness that one's act will bring about a harmful consequence is blameworthy.

   B. Intent

   C. Knowledge

III. Defenses

   A. Self-defense

   B. Insanity

> **TIP:** The best way to determine whether your outline is organized "correctly" is to try a few practice questions. We suggest that you complete a section of your outline on your own, organize a small study group (no more than 2 or 3 persons), and try to answer a sample exam question using only your outlines. You should all work separately and then come together as a group to compare your answers. If you find that your outline contains too much or not enough information, you can revise it before the final exam.

Note that the outlines included in this chapter are not the only way to organize material. The outlines are provided as a guide to organizing material in a way that allows you to learn the law and to prepare for the exam. Remember that all students learn differently, and that you must approach material in a way that works best for you. If, after reading this chapter and attempting to outline, you feel that outlining is not for you, consider flowcharting (see Chapter 6). The important thing is that you take all the information you've read and discussed in class and construct an overview of the material.

Endnotes

1. For more on flowcharts, see Chapter 7.

2. One study found that first year law students who achieved high grades were more likely to use systematic and organized techniques in preparing for classes and exams than their lower-achieving classmates. The study specifically cited creating outlines as one of these techniques. Michael J. Patton, *The Student, the Situation, and Performance During the First Year of Law School*, 21 J. Legal Educ. 10, 21–27 (1967).

3. Lexis.com and Westlaw.com provide a wealth of resources and material for law students and lawyers. Most research services are free to law students while in school, whereas lawyers and law firms pay for certain electronic resources that they offer.

4. This is based on *Lucy v. Zehmer*, 196 Va. 493, 84 S.E.2d 516 (1954).

5. This is based on *Embry v. Hargadine, McKittrick Dry Goods Co.*, 105 S.W. 777 (Mo. Ct. App. 1907).

6. This is based on *Dickinson v. Dodd*, 2 Ch. D. 463 (C.A. 1876).

7. This is based on *Martin v. State*, 17 So.2d 427 (Ala. Civ. App. 1944).

8. This is based on *People v. Newton*, 72 Misc. 2d 646, 340 N.Y.S.2d 77 (1973).

9. This is based on *People v. Decina*, 2 N.Y.2d 133, 138 N.E.2d 799 (1856).

Chapter 7

Putting It Together,
Part Three: Flowcharting

Do you tend to think in terms of the big picture? Do you sometimes think, "I wonder how X relates to Y and how Y relates to Z?" If so, then flowcharting may be more beneficial to you than outlining. A flowchart is analogous to a set of directions or instructions. Going back to our travel analogy, if you were to travel by car to a friend's house, he might give you a map with the route marked. The map would illustrate your starting point and also illustrate where to go, and most importantly, how to get there. Like a map, a flowchart can tell you where you are (on an exam), where you need to go (what issues you should discuss next), and how to get there (what to include in your discussion of those issues). Just as a map points the way on the road, a flowchart points the way on an exam. A flowchart will help you maintain your focus on the exam by reminding you of the issues covered in class.

Do you synthesize information by writing it out? Or, when learning, does it help you to visually see how all the information is inter-related? If so, then creating a flowchart could be an excellent way for you to learn how the elements of the rule fit together in a way that is instructional rather than informational.

What Is a Flowchart?

A flowchart is a diagram or map that shows a progression or a procedure. Flowcharts in law school can explain how various issues and rules are connected and how to answer a law school exam in a step-by-step process. Making a flowchart can help you see the big picture and how all the information fits together. The outline collected all of your information. The flowchart tells you how to get somewhere using that information and puts it in a manageable visual format. As a visual illustration, a flowchart literally draws a picture of how to approach a legal problem.

Do I Have to Create Both a
Flowchart and an Outline?

Some people are uncomfortable making flowcharts. Others don't need to make them because they keep their outline in their head, or they see the flowchart as a repetition of their outline. Also, some classes are not easily divided into sections and questions that go from "If yes, then A, if no, then B." Keep in mind, however, that some **parts** of a class may be difficult for you, and it will be very beneficial to you to flowchart those particular concepts. For example, Real Property as a whole is not easy to flowchart, but its individual sections, such as landlord tenant law, running covenants, and easements are. Thus, you can flowchart landlord-tenant, running covenants, and easements separately, in addition to creating an outline. Although you will undoubtedly become intimately acquainted with these terms by the end of the course, a flowchart will make it easier to picture them and easier to learn them.

How Do I Know If a Flowchart Will Help Me?

A flowchart is especially helpful for visual learners. A visual learner is one who processes information by using pictures, graphs, charts or other pictorial representation. For example, if you used charts and diagrams to answer the word problems on the LSAT, you may be a visual learner. For visual learners, an outline, which is a linear set of instructions, may not be the best way to organize material. Instead, a visual "map," or flowchart, is the best way to demonstrate the relationship of smaller concepts to one another and to the whole. Accordingly, some students should prepare a flowchart, instead of an outline, when it is time to synthesize material. For others, a flowchart supplements an outline. Whereas the outline might be more detailed, a flowchart is a broader depiction of the course, reduced to one page.

What Are the Different Types of Flowcharts?

Remember that flowcharts are like a set of directions or instructions. You can either follow a map to your destination or follow a set of written instructions delineating the correct path to follow. Similarly, flowcharts usually exist in one of two formats: graphic or text-based. The most typical is the graphic format, in which information is included in boxes with lines designating the relationship between the information in the boxes (see example 1). The other common type of flowchart does not utilize graphics connected together but reads more like a set of instructions (see example 2). It leads one through the analysis and poses the questions to ask as one dissects a problem.

Example 1—Graphic Flowchart: Torts

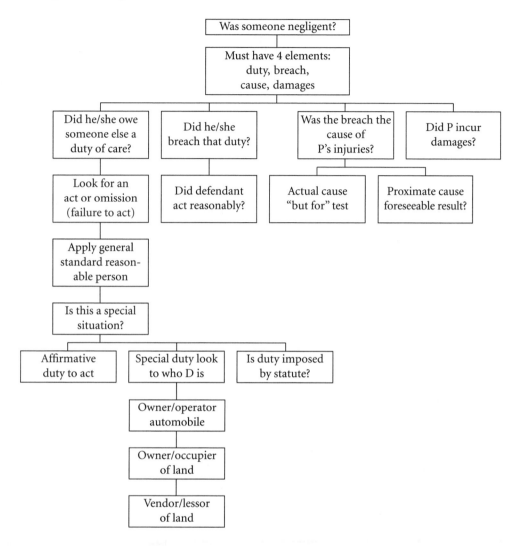

Example 2—Text-Based Flowchart: Torts

Has someone been **negligent**? Must have four things: 1) **Duty,** 2) **Breach,** 3) **Cause, and** 4) **Damages**

1) Did someone owe a **duty** of care to another? Was there a duty? Look for:

   a) an act or an omission (failure to act)

   b) general standard—that of a reasonable person—applies to all—children, people with disabilities, etc.

   c) What was the scope of duty?

      1) ordinary situations—foreseeability of reasonable person of injury to another

      2) special situations

    a)   affirmative duty to act, *e.g.*, duty to control third persons (parent-child), duty to protect third persons (jailer, innkeeper, etc.)

    b)   duties imposed by statute, *e.g.*, Good Samaritan laws

    c)   special duties for owners and operators of automobiles

    d)   special duties for vendors and lessors of land

    e)   special duties for owners and occupiers of land

        1)   to persons outside of land—not to create unreasonable risk of harm

        2)   to persons coming on land—look to see who person is—different rules for adult trespassers, children, frequent intruders, licensees, and invitees

2)   If there is a duty—was there a **breach**?—in light of duty owed—did D act reasonably?

3)   Was the breach the **cause** of P's injuries?

    Look at:

    a)   Actual cause—"but for" test

    b)   Proximate cause—look at foreseeability of what occurred and how it occurred

4)   Did plaintiff incur **damages**?

What Should a Good Flowchart Include?

A good flowchart can lead you through an exam question, making sure that you cover **all** possible issues each question raised. Just like a checklist, you cannot go forward in your answer to a question until you have explored every possible situation or exception to the rule delineated in the flowchart. A flowchart should help you memorize the law, and crucial questions to ask, or the critical issues to cover. A flowchart should "take you through" an exam question. If it does not help, then it needs to be re-written. A flowchart will help even with a closed book exam; however, key phrases and buzz words should be more concise to facilitate memorization prior to the exam.

How to Make Your Own Flowchart

When creating an outline, you focused on the big picture. You must determine how the rules fit together and interact as a whole. A flowchart helps you visualize the big picture and create steps to follow to make all possible arguments on an exam. Creating a flowchart can be done in three easy steps. After explaining the steps, we've included some sample flowcharts to help you understand the flowcharting process.

Step 1—Brainstorm: create a list of all the key words, phrases, and rules that come to mind.

Consider an entire course or part of the course you've covered so far. Write down on a large piece of paper (or, on the computer screen) words and phrases that constantly recur in class (duty, act, omission, minor, negligence), including case names, if any stick in your mind. At this stage, DO NOT sort the information. In other words, write down anything that comes to mind: do not discount anything or arrange items in any order. You are only brainstorming at this point. Try to complete this step without looking at your notes or casebook. Do not write in complete sentences. Just jot down words, phrases, ideas, and names. For example, if you were brainstorming for a contracts class, your brainstorm sheet might look like:

Example of Brainstorm Sheet: Contracts

> Offer
>
> Consideration
>
> Termination of offer
>
> Termination by passage of time
>
> Promise
>
> Offer must have clear and definite terms
>
> Counter-offer
>
> Acceptance
>
> Rejection
>
> Offeror
>
> Offeree
>
> Communication
>
> Bargain for exchange
>
> Commitment
>
> Legal detriment
>
> Silence as acceptance
>
> Waiver as acceptance

Notice that nothing in this brainstorm sheet is put in a particular order or sequence. This particular brainstorm sheet has no case names. It might be that this professor does not require the class to include specific case names on her exam, in which case, the specific names of the cases should not appear on the brainstorm sheet. After you've completed the initial brainstorm sheet, go back and add to it, using your class notes. Again, do not write sentences or attempt to add complete case briefs. Limit yourself to words, or, at most, phrases. If you have already completed an outline and are using a flowchart as a supplement, go through the outline and use it for filling in the brainstorming sheet. The same rule applies: do not attempt to include in the flowchart every word that is in the outline.

TIP: Once you've completed your brainstorm sheet, compare it to one prepared by another. Indeed, this is a great activity for a study group. Rather than using time in the study group to prepare one brainstorm sheet, come together after working individually to compare brainstorm sheets. In this way, each member of the group can add the concepts or phrases they missed to his or her own sheet. Although there is no such thing as a right or wrong brainstorm sheet, by comparing your work with others, you should get a sense of what points and concepts are the most important ones.

Step 2—Organize: separate these terms into different sections/categories.

Now that you have a fairly complete brainstorm sheet, it's time to begin organizing the concepts. Begin by grouping similar concepts or ideas together. For example, you might highlight all the words and phrases dealing with "offer" in yellow and all those on "acceptance" in pink. At this stage, do a fairly broad sort. If you don't know where to begin, look back to the table of contents in your casebook or your syllabus. What broad concepts do those sources identify? If the Contracts casebook begins with: I. Meeting of the Minds: Offer, Acceptance, and Consideration, then you should begin sorting the items in your brainstorm sheet in three groups: offer, acceptance, consideration. Again, this might be an ideal exercise for a study group.

Example: Organize Terms Part One

Offer

> Promise
>
> Commitment
>
> Offer must have clear and definite terms
>
> Offeror
>
> Offeree
>
> Termination of offer
>
> Termination by passage of time
>
> Rejection
>
> Counter-offer

Acceptance

> Communication
>
> Silence as acceptance
>
> Waiver as acceptance

Consideration

> Bargain for exchange
>
> Legal detriment

As you begin to sort items according to broad categories, revise your brainstorm sheet, or create a new list. Rather than present a broad list of items, your sheet should now have some divisions. Notice that this revised list not only has divisions but also subdivisions. You can certainly do this by creating an outline form or visually grouping, using highlighters and shapes to separate distinct concepts.

Example: Organize Terms: Part Two

Offer

> Promise and/or commitment
>
> Offer must have clear and definite terms
>
> Termination of offer
>
>> By Offeror
>>
>> By Offeree
>>
>>> Termination by passage of time
>>>
>>> Rejection
>>>
>>> Counter-offer

Acceptance

> Acceptance must be communicated
>
>> Exceptions:
>>
>> Silence as acceptance
>>
>> Waiver as acceptance

Consideration

> Bargain for exchange
>
> Legal detriment

TIP: Warning!!!!! Notice how the offer grouping in this example is far more involved than the acceptance division. Take this as a warning! Either the acceptance section was not discussed in detail in class or, more likely, this particular student missed some key concepts in this area. If one topic has several items listed under it and another has only a few, you should review your outline or notes. Did you miss listing some items in this category? Was this category not discussed in as much detail as the previous ones? At this stage in the process, you are trying to sort items not only into broad categories, but, if possible, subcategories as well. In this example there are a lot of words listed under offer and now you, the student, need to go back and try to subdivide these terms further. This type of subdivision will help at the next flowcharting stage where you begin to organize the smaller pieces of the puzzle.

Step 3 — Go with the flow: decipher the relationship between the rules and turn these into issues and questions.

In step three, you must figure out the steps you need to take to analyze an exam problem on this issue. To go back to our travel metaphor, you need to draft clear directions so you can "travel" through all the important steps on your exam. If you were writing instructions to explain to a friend how to get to your house, you need to figure out where he would start. Where does he live? What street should he take to get to the highway? Should he go East or West (or North or South)? What exit should he take? Etc.

To figure out what comes first, start with the broadest concept. For example, we noted that your professor might have divided the Contracts course into three areas or issues: offer, acceptance, and consideration. Consider the relationship among the broad concepts first. Do they follow a particular order? In other words, does offer have to come before consideration? Why does one concept come before another? You cannot begin to fill in your flowchart until you have a clear understanding of the relationship among the bigger concepts. "Where do you get this information?" you ask. From your notes! If you have been discussing cases and hypotheticals in class, you need to figure out how the court analyzes each Contracts case. What does it analyze first, second, etc.? Does your professor require that you discuss offer before you discuss acceptance? If so, then you must put offer in your flowchart before acceptance. In our Contracts example, we noted that our list was now divided into three sub-categories: offer, acceptance, and consideration. Now our flowchart begins to take on shape:

Example 2 — Graphics Flowchart: Contracts

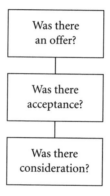

Once you've analyzed the relationship among the broad concepts and have them in some sort of order, you can begin flowcharting each broad concept individually. In other words, your Contracts flowchart begins with offer, then acceptance, and finally consideration. Now, take the offer section. Ask yourself, what do I have to ask myself in determining whether there is an offer on the exam? What steps must I go through? Look back to your sort list (Step 2). Of all the items on the list, what comes first? Why? What happens when it is not present? Where do you go from there?

Notice that each step in the flowchart is posed as a question. This way, you are prompted on what to look for when analyzing an exam question. First, you must discuss whether there is an offer. Ask yourself, "What do I look for here?" Each question should lead to another question. When making a flowchart be as concrete as possible. Do not include "directions" like "look for an offer"—what does this mean? Break it down into specific requirements or elements. List specific concrete steps, rather than vague abstract ones. Notice how the following sample flowchart for offer is much more concrete than the previous example:

Sample Graphics Flowchart—Contracts

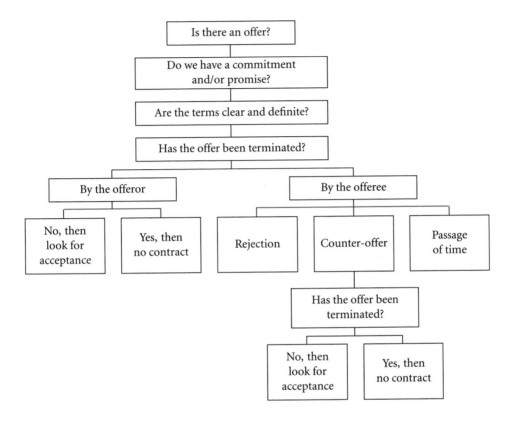

Other Alternatives

As we noted previously, you might flowchart, instead of outlining, or you might flowchart, in addition to outlining. If you choose to flowchart, instead of creating an outline, you may find that graphics, boxes, and colors help depict the relationship among the concepts. If you found outlining very useful, then you might not benefit from graphics. Instead, you might need what we call a linear flowchart, like the text-based flowchart shown here.

Sample Text-based Flowchart—Contracts

Is there an offer?

    Do we have a commitment or a promise?

    Are the terms clear and definite?

Has the offer been terminated?—No, then look for acceptance.

    By the offeror

    By the offeree

Did he reject the offer?

Did he let the time for acceptance lapse?

Did he make a counter-offer?

If you do everything on your laptop computer, you might want to seek out software to help you put your flowchart in electronic format. There are many different programs at your disposal; we will discuss a couple of them to get you thinking about which one might work best for you. There are three flowcharting software programs that we will discuss, but remember that there may be many more options out there, so make sure to do a bit of research before you commit to a specific program.

TIP: When considering flowcharting software see if you can …

1. Try it free for 30 days. Most software companies have free trial periods and you should use it to really determine if this software is worth your money.

2. Transfer the material to a written outline or word processing software, like Microsoft Word. This could be helpful in creating an outline.

3. Use it easily and efficiently. If you find that you have difficulty changing the colors or the links or graphs, it might take up too much of your time and it might not be worth it.

The first program is Inspiration. It can be found online at http://inspiration.com. This is flowcharting software designed to help you put your ideas into a chart. The program allows you to color-code different parts of the outline. You can add pictures from its picture library, and it is easy to click and drag concepts to different parts of the chart. You can also add notes to any part of the flowchart and the notes will appear when you click on that portion of the chart. Finally, you can click a button and convert the chart into a skeletal outline. Any notes that you added will be incorporated into the outline and can assist you if you prefer to prepare your flowchart before you draft an outline.

The second program is Rationale. It is available at http://austhink.com. Rationale is a bit different in that the focus is on creating a chart with reasoning. In Rationale you will make if/then arguments or statements linked with the word because. Rationale transfers your chart into essay format into a word processor, such as Microsoft Word.

The third program is MindManager and is sold online at http://mindjet.com. Mind-Manager is different from the other two programs in that you focus on the concept first and the program will help you organize your thoughts. MindManager integrates directly with Microsoft Office and appears to be geared towards corporations and used for managing projects and people on teams.

Even though we have included three different options, there are other options available. The key is to research the available software and find what works best for you. Make sure that the software helps you organize your thoughts and does not hinder your progress of understanding the material.

Final Thoughts

Both outlining and flowcharting are tools you can use to learn the law and learn how everything you've discussed fits together. You may want to use one or both of these tools. The important thing is to organize in a way that works. There is no one "right" way to approach learning (or, for that matter, practicing) the law. Start early and try different approaches and methods. We've included some sample flowcharts (and the steps we went through to create them) for your use. **CAVEAT:** these examples might not fit your particular course or professor! In fact, the flowcharts that follow include only one topic in each subject and are not comprehensive. They may, however, be a place for you or your study group to start in terms of putting together your own flowcharts. Good luck!

Sample Flowcharts

Constitutional Law — Equal Protection

Step 1 — Brainstorm.

Equal protection

Classification

Suspect

Discriminatory in effect

Rational basis

Governmental action

Injury

Strict scrutiny

Discriminatory on its face

Intermediate scrutiny

14th amendment

Standing

Step 2 — Organize.

Do we have an Equal Protection violation?

    A   If x is entitled to a right, then y, who is similarly situated to x, is also entitled to the same right

    B.   Plaintiff must have standing

    C.   Injury must have come from the governmental action

D. How is the government classifying people?

   1. Suspect: race, ethnicity

      a. Suspect on its face

         i.   Apply strict scrutiny

         ii. Must be necessary to achieve a compelling governmental interest

      b. In effect—discriminatory purpose

         i.   If yes, apply strict scrutiny

         ii. If no, apply rationale basis

   2. Quasi-Suspect: gender

      a. On its face

         i.   Apply intermediate scrutiny

         ii. Must be substantially related to an important governmental end

      b. In effect—look to intent

         i.   If discriminatory intent, apply intermediate scrutiny

         ii. If no discriminatory intent, apply rationale basis

   3. Non-Suspect: economic, age

      a. Apply rationale basis

      b. Need to have a rationale relationship between the classification and some legitimate governmental purpose

Step 3—Go with the flow.

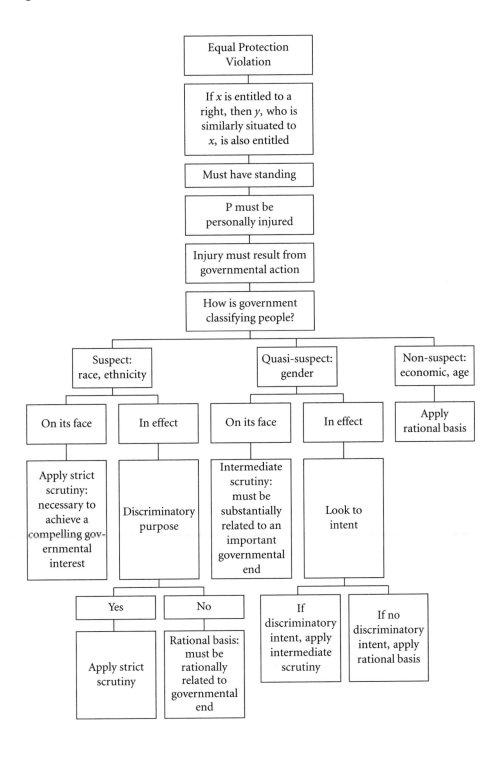

Civil Procedure—Pleadings

Step 1—Brainstorm.

Jurisdiction

Sanctions

Cross-claim

Counter-claim

Third-party claim

Fraud or mistake must be pled with particularity

Filed in "good faith"—Rule 11

Complaint

Answer

Filed in a timely manner

Demand for relief

Venue

Short & plain statement

12(b)(6)

Service of process

Affirmative defenses

Step 2—Organize.

1) Have you been asked to analyze a **complaint**? Look for common flaws, including:
   a) short and plain statement of claim
   b) demand for relief
   c) statement of jurisdiction/venue
   d) failure to plead a special matter w/particularity
   e) failure to investigate basis of complaint
   f) not filed in a timely manner

2) A complaint has been filed and it's the defendant's turn to respond. Try and see if you can file a **motion**. Motions to choose from include:
   a) lack of personal jurisdiction
   b) lack of subject matter jurisdiction/venue
   c) failure to state a claim
   d) insufficiency of process
   e) insufficiency of service of process

3) Rather than filing a motion, defendant files an **answer**. Two issues to look for:
   a) by filing an answer instead of a motion, has D **waived** anything? (make sure you know which of the above motions are waived if not raised right away)

   b) are there any **problems with the answer?**

      1) was it filed in good faith?

      2) does it include affirmative defenses?

      3) should D include a cross-, counter-, or third-party claim?

Step 3 — Go with the flow.

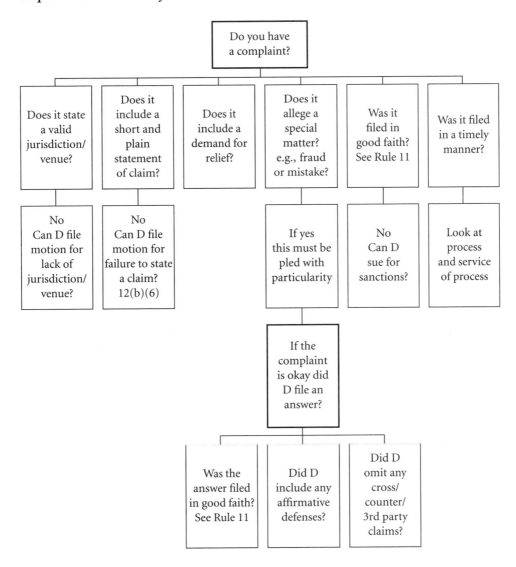

Criminal Law

Step 1 — Brainstorm.

Actus reus — act

Mens rea — mental state

Omission — failure to act when you should act

Model penal code

Common law

Knowledge

Intentional

Voluntary act

Defenses

Infancy

Necessity

Statute

Assumption — you started to act, now you must finish

Peril — you put a person in peril — you must act to help him or her

Relationship

Purposeful

Consent

Reckless

Negligence

Mistake

Strict liability

Malice

Willful

Contract

Causation

Excuse

Entrapment

General intent

Specific intent

Step 2 — Organize.

Actus reus — act

    Voluntary act

    Omission — failure to act when you should act because of SCRAP:

        Statute

        Contract

        Relationship

        Assumption — you started to act, now you must finish

        Peril — you put a person in peril — you must act to help him or her

Mens rea — mental state

    Model penal code

        Purposeful

        Knowledge

        Reckless

        Negligence

        Strict liability

    Common law

        General intent

        Specific intent

        Malice

        Intentional

        Willful

Causation

Defenses

    Mistake

    Necessity

    Excuse

    Infancy

    Entrapment

    Consent

Step 3 — Go with the flow.

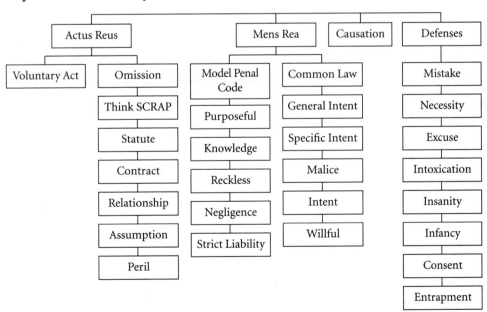

Chapter 8

Law School Examinations

Law students begin school like travelers begin a journey, excited by the prospect of meeting new people, learning new things, and pursuing a life dream. After two months of reading cases, attending classes, and drafting legal writing papers, most law students, like weary travelers, start longing for the days when their surroundings were familiar and they felt self-assured and confident in their abilities. Law students usually experience this "homesickness" when, after two months or so of school, they find themselves confused about the readings and class discussions, and unsure about how all the information fits together. Rather than exude confidence about upcoming exams, law students express fear. While some of the fear can be alleviated with outlining and flow-charting, the prospect of the exam itself is daunting. Knowing the goals and purposes of the exam and exactly what is expected of students and having a process to use in attacking the exam are empowering. This chapter introduces the what, why, and how of law school exams, and points out some of the most typical types of exams. The next chapter will provide tools for conquering homesickness for the way things were, and for forging ahead to the great soon-to-be known.

What Should I Expect on My Law School Exams?

Contrary to common belief, law school exams do not require you to repeat class discussion verbatim or repeat the facts of every case you read. Although your professor might have demanded that students understand each detail of every case for class discussion, her exam might not require you to know a single case name. Thus, students who prepare for the exam by memorizing each and every detail of the cases covered in class are not studying the right material. No law school exam question will ever ask: "We have discussed the *Vosburg* case in detail in this course. Tell me everything you know about this case." Instead, the law school exam will test your understanding of the rule that evolved from the *Vosburg* case, and your ability to apply that rule to a new set of facts.

Most undergraduate courses test comprehension, memorization, and, to a degree, analysis. Most law school exams test primarily analysis or application. Although memorization and comprehension are necessary to do well on an exam, memorization and comprehension alone are not sufficient. To succeed on an exam, students must problem-solve. While no law school exam will ask you to repeat any one lecture, let alone one case, you will be required to dissect a fact pattern, identify the issues, articulate the rules of law, and apply those rules to this fact situation. The same dissection skills you practiced while you briefed cases are those you will use when answering a law school exam question. Knowing that you will be tested on your problem-solving skills and your ability to think like a lawyer, you might still wonder: "What will my exam look like?"

Most law school exams are somewhat similar to cases. There might be a long (*e.g.*, one page) or a short (*e.g.*, five sentences) fact pattern with either a few or many persons with problems. This will be presented in a basic fact scenario of "what happened." You will have a story of different people doing different things, and at the end, some people will suffer some loss. You must determine which party or parties will win in court. Let's review the sample exam question we first presented in Chapter 1.

Sample Law School Exam Question

Thirteen-year-old Bobby, the school bully, beat up on Steven and Jamal, also thirteen, every day. Unable to take it anymore, Steven and Jamal went to the school cafeteria to talk to Steven's older brother, Kevin, about how to stop Bobby. Steven reminded Kevin that he still owed them a favor for their help with his science project a month ago. Kevin, eighteen, agreed to "take care" of Bobby for Steven and Jamal, but only if they gave Kevin their allowance for the next six months. Both Steven and Jamal agreed. Just to be sure, Jamal snatched a napkin to record the agreement, and all three signed it at the bottom.

The next day at school, Steven and Jamal were called into the principal's office and informed that Bobby was in the hospital with a broken nose and a broken arm. Afraid of the consequences, Steven and Jamal refused to pay Kevin his "fee." Since Kevin cannot afford a lawyer on his allowance, he has come to you and wants to know if he can get his "fee" from Steven and Jamal.

You may have noticed that this exam question does not mention any cases or rules from cases. Now you may be saying to yourself, "I can't answer that!" or "How does my professor expect me to answer this exam? We never did anything like this before. Why am I being tested this way?" This method of testing is not random; there are many reasons why the traditional law school exam exists in this format.

Why Am I Being Tested This Way?

The traditional law school exam tests your ability to solve problems and think like a lawyer. Unless your client is a lawyer, she will not be able to tell you what she wants to sue for, what arguments to make on her behalf, or even whom she can sue. Instead, a client will come into your office with a problem, and she won't know what to do. She may inundate you with more facts than you need, or may not give you enough facts. You will have to sort out the facts to determine the specific issue or problem at hand. Then you will have to apply the law to these facts to determine whether your client has a viable lawsuit. The overall goal of law school is to train you to think like a lawyer. Exams are the primary way of creating training simulations that reflect real lawyer-client relationships, albeit under intense time constraints. It is important to learn to break down the problem or hypothetical until all possible legal issues are clear. Once you have learned to do that, then you can take the next step to decide what actions to take on each separate issue.

How Does the Exam Relate to Class Discussion?

Although the two may seem miles apart, class discussion and the exam are closely related. As you prepare for class discussion, you read cases carefully, concentrating on dissecting the relevant facts, isolating the issue, distilling the rules, and articulating the court's reasoning. When you participate in class discussion, you not only check your understanding of all of the parts of the case, but your professor also challenges you to apply your understanding to different fact situations by posing hypotheticals. The exam itself is an extension of class discussion. On an exam, the hypotheticals are longer, more complex, and written, but they challenge you to engage in problem solving, just like in-class oral hypotheticals. Professors give hypotheticals in class to teach you the way they want you to learn and to approach the case from their specific legal point of view. Make it a point to write down at least one hypothetical for each issue you discuss in class; that way you have a basis of what the exam will cover.

Different Types of Law School Exams

Most law school exams test problem-solving skills. There are different ways to test these skills. Earlier, we introduced you to the concept of IRAC-spotting the issue, articulating the rule, applying or analyzing the rule in the context of new or unfamiliar facts, and reaching a conclusion about the likely outcome of the problem—when we introduced case briefing (IRAC is FIRAC without the facts). The same concept can be used on exams. One way to solve problems on a law school exam is to use IRAC (we will go into more detail about IRAC in the next chapter), but most professors do not treat all parts of IRAC equally. Depending on the type of exam, you may need to focus in on one part of IRAC more than others.

There are three different types of law school exams: (1) issue-spotting, (2) analysis, and (3) policy. Some professors have different methods in which they require their students to answer a question. For instance, on an offer issue on a Contracts exam, a professor may tell her students to assume that a valid offer exists and to answer only the acceptance part of the question. It is very important that you follow the directions given by your professor and answer **only** the question asked. It is important to find out how your professor wants his or her exam questions answered.

TIP: To figure out what to expect from your professor on an exam, try the following:

1) Find out if your professor keeps old exams on reserve in the library or posted on the school's webpage and check them out. **CAUTION:** Your professor always has the right to change his or her testing format and can do so at any time.

2) Ask 2nd and 3rd year students about your professor's exams.

3) Go directly to the source: ask the professor yourself. If this last choice seems daunting, make an appointment and take a few friends with you. Most professors are happy to meet with students eager to do well in their course.

Issue-Spotting

Certain professors test differently because their learning goals for the class vary. In other words, a professor might set as a goal that by the end of the course each student will be able to identify the relevant issues in a complicated fact pattern, articulate the rule, and be able to apply the rule before moving on to the next issue. This professor will devote much class time to discussing cases. Once the class has mastered the information, the professor will then pose hypotheticals to test students' understanding. This professor likely will give an issue-spotting exam. This type of exam is analogous to looking at a person quickly and then describing as much about her as possible: looks, clothes, features, etc. In other words, the exam will require you to go through a complicated fact pattern and identify all the issues triggered by the facts. Once an issue has been identified, you must then articulate the rules governing this type of issue and quickly apply the rules to the fact situation at hand. The arduous task in this type of examination is recognizing which facts trigger which issues and presenting a short and concise analysis of each issue found.

Analysis

Other professors set different goals. They expect a student to explore a single issue in-depth, rather than evaluate several issues briefly. Exploring an issue in depth requires articulating both main and opposing arguments and identifying flaws in each side's presentation. There might not be a lot of issues to discuss, but those that are significant should be explored fully. In this instance, the professor has set as a goal "critical thinking." Because this professor wants his class to master analytical thinking skills, a lot of class time is spent exploring individual cases in great detail and working through problems and hypotheticals in great depth. In the classroom, students may spend a few days or even a week discussing a single case or issue. Here, issue-spotting is not a primary learning goal; critical reasoning is. This type of exam is analogous to looking at a person and then being asked to describe in detail a single item of clothing he is wearing. The exam here, regardless of form, will require you to do more than articulate one or two sentences of analysis before turning to the next issue. You must focus on both sides of the argument and fully critique them.

Policy-Oriented

Other professors might set yet another type of learning goal. Rather than focus on students' ability to dissect cases and spot issues or apply the rule to the facts in a well-reasoned way, this professor wants to see the class master abstract thinking. In other words, the class should learn not only what the law is and how it is applied, but should be able to question the result as well. A student should be able to understand the rationale underlying the rule. This kind of thinking is most often facilitated in the classroom with discussion about policy and theory. There might not be a lot said about specific cases, but there probably is quite a bit of discussion about whether the result in a particular case was sound and whether the case can be categorized by a particular legal theory. The exam in this type of class is likely to assess whether you can analyze a problem using theory and policy as a guide. On this type of exam, you must not only know why the rule was adopted, but you must also be able to present the arguments against the rule. On this kind of exam, you should be prepared to argue the theory and policy both for and against the rule. This shows comprehension and acknowledgement of the complexity of the rule.

Some professors have multiple learning goals for their students and may give an exam with a combination of any of the three different types we've discussed. Such an exam, for example, might involve short answer or multiple-choice questions for issue spotting and essay questions for analysis and policy. Regardless of your professor's goal, and regardless of the type of exam your professor gives, all law school exams share a common thread: they all require problem-solving. The next chapter offers a process for solving law school problems.

Chapter 9

Tips on Exam Preparation

By now you should be a bit more familiar with why law schools test in a particular way, and what the goals of the examination are. Familiarity with the exam is not enough. To succeed, you need a process—an approach—for taking the exam. Which process you use is vital. It's like selecting the right tool for the job, or the right accessories for your trip. If you are going hiking or camping, you need a good backpack that is easy to pack, can hold all your stuff, and can fit on your back. This backpack would be essential for tackling the mountains or the great outdoors. For your law school journey, you need a powerful tool to use to tackle your law school exams.

Process of Problem Solving

You have to choose a strategy for tackling the exam that will lead you to some resolution. In mathematics, for example, different formulas are used to analyze different types of problems. Likewise, in law, a particular formula is used to analyze all legal problems: IRAC (remember, IRAC is FIRAC without the facts). Using IRAC will not guarantee an A, but it will help you organize your responses in a way that makes sense and impresses your professor. The process is especially helpful when answering long and short essay questions, and is useful for closed book, open book, and take-home exams. IRAC is **NOT** the only process or mechanism for answering law school exams (indeed, you may need to modify the formula to meet your needs), but it is a good start to help facilitate "thinking like a lawyer."

IRAC for Examinations

You may remember IRAC from our earlier chapter on reading and briefing cases. We introduced IRAC, or more specifically FIRAC, as a method for briefing cases. You can use that same method for answering law school exams. Go through the IRAC process for each and every issue you identify on an exam.

I — Identify the Issues

Your first task is to "spot the issues" or figure out the specific rules involved in the fact pattern. To spot issues, you need to skim the question once and identify the big general issues that leap out at you (battery, assault, etc.). Then go back, read the entire question, and zero in on the precise sub-issues involved. For example, don't stop once you've identified a battery issue. Battery is too general to be conclusive. Instead, the real "I" in this case is the sub-issue. Battery is defined as the *intentional*, *harmful* or *offensive touching* of a *person*. This definition has three elements or sub-issues: (1) intentional, (2) harmful or offensive touching, and (3) person. A fact pattern may contain one or more of these sub-issues. The most important thing to do is read the question and/or fact pattern very carefully. Finally, after you've read over a question once and identified the big issues, you need to re-read the question with a more careful eye. As you read, pause after every sentence and evaluate the relevance of the facts in that sentence. Think: what issue(s) do the facts in this sentence trigger? Can these facts be used in a main or opposing argument? Realize that a professor usually intends **EVERY** single word in a fact pattern to be pertinent. Professors usually do not include extraneous words on an exam. You should remember that each fact in a question probably has some relevancy and should not be discounted. Let's look at an example.

Sample Law School Exam Question

Gus Oontite is a diligent law student. He was horrified when, after a month of flu-like symptoms, his doctor informed him that he had a rare type of mononucleosis (mono) that may or may not be contagious. The doctor advised Gus to stay away from people. Gus refused, and went to school the next day. He made it through the morning without sneezing. While eating lunch in the cafeteria, Gus spotted his enemy, Connie Tagious. Connie sat across from Gus and began taunting him about his red nose and watery eyes. Gus, unable to bear anymore, began playing with the salt and pepper from the shakers on the table as a distraction from Connie's insults. Unfortunately, the pepper began to tickle Gus's nose. As he felt himself about to sneeze, he grabbed for his handkerchief. Connie turned away and Gus sneezed on the torts book Connie was holding. Although Connie did not suffer any immediate injury, she came down with a mild cold about a week later. Discuss Connie's claims.

Where would you start with this hypothetical? First, you would have to spot the issues. Always work your way from the biggest to the smallest issues. In this case, we would begin by identifying this as a torts case. Specifically, this is intentional torts. Even more specifically, this is a battery claim. To analyze battery, you will need to discuss (1) whether Gus intended to harm or offend Connie, (2) whether Connie suffered harmful or offensive contact, and (3) whether the sneezing on the book was contact with Connie's person.

R—Articulate the Rules

After you have identified the issue, you must articulate the rules. For each sub-issue you identify, you need to go through the IRAC process. If the sub-issue is battery/intent, the rules you will be expected to articulate are those that pertain to the intent element of battery. What is the definition of battery? What must a plaintiff prove to satisfy the intent element of battery? You do not have to cite cases (unless your professor says otherwise). Instead, at this stage focus on articulating rules that clearly and precisely define the element or sub-issue you are writing about. The answer to our Connie v. Gus problem so far would look like this:

> Connie can successfully sue Gus for battery if she can prove the three elements of battery: (1) intent, (2) harmful or offensive contact, and (3) with the person of another. Connie can satisfy the intent element if she can prove that Gus desired the end result of his conduct (to give her a disease) or if it is substantially certain that Connie would become ill as a result of his sneeze.

A—Apply the Rules to the Facts

Here is the most challenging part of IRAC. Having articulated the rule pertaining to the sub-issue, you need to apply the rule to the facts and make arguments for BOTH sides. What does this mean? This means that you need to tell the professor whether or not the facts support the particular element you are dealing with. You must constantly answer the question "why?" The key word here is "because." For example, on a battery question with the key issue of intent, you must focus on why there is or is not sufficient intent for a battery. Explain the existence of the element using the facts in the question. Why is there a battery? "Because there is intent." Why is there intent? "Because it was substantially certain that if defendant sneezed on the book he would pass his germs and his illness on to the plaintiff." Strive to create a sentence structured in the same manner: "The element of intent is present because [state those facts that prove this element]...."

Whenever possible, make sure to present the opposing argument. You not only want to articulate why one party should win (because there is intent), but you also want to tell your professor what the opposition will say. Once you explain WHY the facts of the question show that intent is present, you must then say that the other side will argue "there is no intent because ..." Again, you want to use the facts to support your statement. Although the process of applying the elements of the rules to the facts looks simple, it is the most difficult part for a law student (and a lawyer) to tackle. Our formula "element is met because of key facts" is oversimplified. Suppose X is caught going forty-five miles per hour in a twenty-five mile per hour speed zone (fact). A statute proscribes that going twenty miles over the speed limit is negligence. How would you apply the law to the facts here? Simply saying: "She was negligent because she was going twenty miles over the speed limit" is not good enough. In fact, that answer is conclusory, meaning it offers no "why." A complete application would say: "The law states that going twenty miles over the speed limit is negligence. In this case, defendant was going forty-five in a twenty-five mph zone—the required twenty miles over the speed limit. Hence, she has been negligent." Your application needs to be this explicit and complete. Unless the question "why" is answered throughout, your application is incomplete. To take Connie and Gus one step further then:

> Connie can sue Gus for battery if she can demonstrate the three elements of battery: (1) intent, (2) harmful or offensive contact, and (3) person of another. Connie can satisfy the intent element if she can prove that Gus desired the end result of his conduct (to give her a disease) or if it was substantially certain that Connie would become ill as a result of his sneeze.
>
> In this case, Connie can argue that Gus intended both his actions (sneezing) and the result (her getting ill) because, viewing Connie as an enemy, he played with the pepper in order to induce a sneeze, which he knew, based on the doctor's warning, would be the type of contact that would spread his mono. Connie can also argue that even if Gus didn't intend to give her mono, he knew with substantial certainty that his sneeze would spread his sickness to others, based on his doctor's telling him to "stay away from people."
>
> Gus will point out, however, that he never meant to give Connie mono. He will argue that although he knew he was contagious, he nonetheless tried to stop his sneeze with a handkerchief. Gus was not substantially certain that sneezing would spread his mono because the doctor only told him that his mono may be contagious.
>
> Gus's argument will probably fail, however, because his doctor told him to stay away from people; thus, he should have been substantially certain that bad consequences could follow his action to expose others.
>
> As to harmful or offensive contact . . .

C—Conclusion

After stating both the main and opposing arguments, you must call a winner. This is the shortest part of IRAC. Although most students think there is a "right" or "wrong" answer, most of the time, the result doesn't really matter. Most professors do not look for a particular conclusion, as long as the arguments of both parties are clearly and completely explained. Moreover, it is fallacious to assume that there is a clear-cut correct answer. More often than not, there is no correct answer. You only need to take a position and defend it.

Take a look at the sample question and answer in IRAC format below.

Sample Exam Question #1—Contracts

Thirteen-year-old Bobby, the school bully, beat up on Steven and Jamal, also thirteen, every day. Unable to take it anymore, Steven and Jamal went to the school cafeteria to talk to Steven's older brother, Kevin, about how to stop Bobby. Steven reminded

Kevin that he still owed them a favor for helping him with his science project a month ago. Kevin, eighteen, agreed to "take care" of Bobby for Steven and Jamal, but only if they agreed to give Kevin their allowance for the next six months. Both Steven and Jamal agreed. Just to be sure, Jamal wrote out the agreement on a napkin and all three signed it at the bottom.

The next day at school, Steven and Jamal were called into the principal's office and informed that Bobby was in the hospital with a broken nose and a broken arm. Afraid of the consequences, Steven and Jamal refused to pay Kevin his "fee." Kevin has come to you and wants to know if he can get his "fee" from Steven and Jamal.

Sample Answer in IRAC format

Issue	The issue in this case is whether or not the contract between Steven and Jamal and Kevin is valid, given that (1) Steven and Jamal are minors (both are thirteen), and (2) the contract is for illegal activity (fighting).
Rule	Any contract signed by a person before reaching the age of majority is voidable by that person. (The age of majority varies from state to state, but it is eighteen in most states). All contracts that call for one or more of the parties to engage in illegal activity are void and not enforceable.
Application	Steven and Jamal can attempt to void the contract *because* they are minors. They can assert that the contract is voidable by them *because* they are both under the age of eighteen, and therefore do not have the capacity to bind themselves to a contract. Steven and Jamal can also argue that, even if they did not want to void the contract because of their incapacity, the contract is automatically void *because* it was illegal. Steven and Jamal can assert that the contract was for an illegal act *because* Kevin was to "take care" of Bobby or beat him up, and Kevin in fact did beat him up to the point of putting him in the hospital with a broken nose and a broken arm.
Conclusion	Because Steven and Jamal are minors and the contract involved illegal activity, the contract is void and cannot be enforced; therefore Kevin will not be able to recover his "fee" from Steven and Jamal.

Here is another example of an exam question and answer written in IRAC format. Review the synthesis example number three from Chapter 4 before reading this question and answer.

Sample Exam Question #2[1] — Property

Tommy One-L just moved to Big City and signed a one-year lease on an apartment on City Avenue. He began his legal studies at Big City University's School of Law in August. As a first-year student, Tommy is fairly high-strung and operates under an enormous amount of stress. He spends countless hours each week preparing for classes and completing his "outside" legal reading. As a student, he finds it especially important that his apartment be a place of refuge. He needs peace and quiet in order to keep on top of his studies, as well as to maintain some semblance of mental health.

About one month after moving into his apartment, Tommy awakened one Saturday morning and entered his kitchen. Turning on the light, Tommy was thunderstruck to discover his apartment overrun by thousands of cockroaches. Horrified and repulsed by the "invasion," he telephoned his landlord, who said he couldn't take care of the problem for at least a week. As a result, Tommy moved out. Moving understandably involved a great deal of time, when time was at a premium for Tommy. After he resettled into his new apartment (which commands substantially higher rent), Tommy's landlord sued him for back rent and other damages. Tommy wants to know whether he has a defense to his landlord's lawsuit.

Sample Answer in IRAC Format

Issue	Whether Tommy can successfully defend an action for back rent based on constructive eviction, due to a large quantity of cockroaches in the apartment.
Rule	Constructive eviction refers to circumstances under the control of the landlord and that compel the tenant to leave the premises, though not asked to leave. In order to assert constructive eviction as a defense to an action for unpaid rent, a tenant must prove that some safety issue or health hazard prevented him or her from living in the apartment. A mere nuisance, such as noise, is insufficient.
Application Main Argument	Tommy can argue that the apartment is unsafe in this situation *because* it is infested with cockroaches. Cockroaches pose both a safety issue and a health hazard *because* they can have serious health consequences for the tenant. Cockroaches carry diseases and can contaminate food. *Because* sickness can spread to the tenant, cockroaches can be viewed as a health hazard. This is similar to the case of an apartment damaged by fire *because* both can lead to the spread of illness. These are similar *because* just as fire damage can lead to breathing unclean air, cockroaches can damage food and spread disease. These situations are similar *because* they both cause health problems. Tommy can also assert that his situation is similar to the case in which an apartment had no heat in the middle of winter. In that case the apartment was unsafe *because* the temperature was below zero, and that could cause the tenants to become sick. In this case, Tommy's apartment was unsafe *because* the infestation of the cockroaches could contaminate the food and cause Tommy to get sick.
Opposing Argument	The landlord will argue that this is merely a nuisance *because* one week is sufficient time to fix the cockroach problem. He will assert that Tommy acted prematurely and did not give the landlord a reasonable amount of time in which to fix the problem. The landlord is wrong; this is not merely a nuisance *because* unlike the case of the loud noise that is only bothersome and has no long-term consequences, cockroaches spread disease quickly and can cause serious health problems.
Conclusion	A court likely will find that Tommy can make a valid constructive eviction defense due to the safety and health issues presented by the cockroaches.

In this second example, the arguments in the analysis are presented for both sides, Tommy and his landlord. Note that this second analysis contains additional information that the first example did not: case analogies and distinctions. In making some arguments (depending on your class and your professor), it might be important to argue that your case is either similar to, or different from, other cases that you discussed in class. This will strengthen your argument, because if your case is just like another that was previously decided a certain way, you can assert that your case should have the same result.

Tips for Different Exam Formats

Now that you know the basic problem-solving method for law school exams, following is some information on the different formats of exams (open versus closed book). Later we will also suggest how to budget and manage your time during an essay exam.

Essay Exams

Closed Book

Closed book is the "traditional" law school examination format and the one most commonly used. In a closed book exam, you are expected to have memorized all the rules, and may not bring anything into the exam other than a pen or pencil.

Whether essay, short answer, or multiple choice, a large part of the challenge here is not only to memorize but truly to understand the law. If you are unable to articulate the rule of law or recognize it in a closed book exam, you will be unable to demonstrate your understanding of the principles. In preparing for a closed book exam, you should do several things.

First, make sure you have the correct principles of law in your outline or flowchart. Have you put the parts together in a way that accurately describes the whole? Do you have a clear understanding of the majority and minority views?

Once you've assured yourself that you put the rules together in a coherent way, you need to memorize them. Prepare flashcards or use those available commercially (caution — the latter are not as accurate as the ones you make yourself because they only summarize the generic rule and are not specific to your professor). Reduce a lengthy outline into a one or two-page summary to memorize. See Chapter 6 on flowcharting. You probably are unable to memorize forty or more pages, but you are able to memorize two pages of information.

> **TIP:** When studying, saying the rules out loud helps you remember much better than reading silently to yourself. This is probably because hearing the rules, even in your own voice, reinforces them in your mind. Your roommates may think you're crazy, but it really works!

At this point, the words and phrases should be so familiar to you that by simply mentioning them, you should be able to fill in the details. Consider using mnemonics.

Create little anagrams or phrases to help you remember concepts. One commonly known phrase is "my legs," a mnemonic in which each of the first letters of the phrase stands for an exception to the statute of frauds in Contracts (marriage, year, land, executor, guaranty, and surety). Remember that although simple memorization is not the key to a good grade, it certainly is a beginning.

Having memorized the rules, you need to make sure that you can apply these principles to new fact situations. Overall, a closed book exam tests three levels of skills: (1) knowledge of rules; (2) understanding the relationship of the subparts to the whole; and (3) ability to apply the rules in problem-solving.

Once you are taking the exam, before you read or even skim any questions, jot down memorized words or phrases on the inside cover of the bluebook or on a piece of scratch paper. This prevents you from forgetting key phrases and helps you read the examination with the main issues in mind. If you cannot remember the exact wording of a rule, paraphrase it as best as you can. You may still score points if your application of the rule is thorough.

Open Book

In an open book exam, students may bring only certain materials (usually a collection of statutes), or any materials (including outlines, flowcharts, etc.) with them to use during the exam. Given the sources available during the exam, memorization is not necessarily one of the skills tested. However, it is crucial to remember that you will not have time to search for the rules at your leisure. Some students, if allowed to bring in an outline, choose to annotate it and include a table of contents. This way, they can quickly locate the relevant rule. An outline or flowchart is still recommended for an open-book examination.

Although rule memorization might not be a part of an open book exam, rule comprehension clearly is tested, as is rule application; therefore, make sure your outline illustrates how all the parts and subparts fit together, and includes supporting cases and hypotheticals. Before you annotate your materials, check with your professor. Some only allow "clean" copies of materials (that is, unmodified), and you risk losing your sources during the exam. If you are allowed to annotate your materials, consider tabbing your code or statute book for quick reference. The biggest mistake students make during an open-book examination is to search aimlessly for a rule or principle. To avoid this, get organized.

Take Home

The take home exam is either loved or loathed. Some students love this format because it does not require memorizing a great deal of information, and it allows time to think, organize, write, edit, and proofread responses. Others loathe the take home exam because it requires full comprehension and application of the law. Although your professor does not expect you to memorize material, she does expect you to understand it and apply it thoroughly and thoughtfully. Whether you choose to prepare an outline or flowchart for the course with a take home exam depends on certain variables. You will have to put together the material you've learned in a way that will facilitate your understanding when you are writing your answers.

Some students decide to outline before the exam to get an overall understanding of the course. Others wait until they receive the exam before putting together the relevant materials into some organized format. A take home examination does not mean a disorganized one! Thoughtfulness, rather than wordiness, is rewarded, so it makes sense to be precise, rather than sloppy. Do not put off the exam until the last minute. Start early. Read each question and develop a task list. How many questions will you answer each day? Which one will you answer first? Once you've selected the question, read it carefully, and consider the issues it raises. What are the relevant guiding legal principles? How do those principles apply in this context? Because of the time frame, check, recheck, and then check again your grammar, citations, punctuation, and spelling. Save and resave regularly to avoid fatal computer crashes. Do not wait until the last minute to print out the finished product; lengthy delays at your school's computer lab are inevitable.

Multiple Choice

All students undoubtedly have taken multiple choice exams, usually on standardized tests, like the LSAT. Although some students prefer the "objective" exam, multiple choice exams are not necessarily easier than essays or short answers. For the most part, multiple choice exams still require students to know the law, understand it, and apply it to different fact situations. The only difference between essay and multiple choice questions is that the answer is provided on multiple choice exams. Given the format of multiple choice questions, students who have studied hard but do not excel at written communication can do very well on multiple choice exams.

There are specific steps in approaching multiple choice exams. First, develop a strategy and stick to it. Whether you choose to read the question first and then read the fact pattern or vice versa, use the same strategy throughout the exam. Second, once you have a strategy in mind, determine how much time is allotted for each question, make a schedule, and stick to it. For example, a multiple choice section worth 25% of the total points on a four-hour exam calls for spending one hour on the multiple choice questions. If the exam has thirty multiple choice questions, and you have an hour to answer them, you can figure two minutes per question. If you find yourself stuck on a question, move on after two minutes and return to it after you have answered the rest of the questions. You can also choose one letter as your default choice to use when you are stuck, and change it when you return to those questions. Third, figure out the answer yourself, and look for it among the options. If you know what the answer is, you won't be fooled by wrong answers that merely "look right." Fourth, if you have overlapping options, dissect the options into individual choices. Overlapping options are those in which the question has more than one answer or combinations of answers, and this is reflected in the options. Following are examples.

Overlapping Options

1. Which of the following does not violate the statute?

    I.   Proposition 1
    II. Proposition 2
    III. Proposition 3

    IV. Proposition 4

    A. I. Only

    B. III. Only

    C. I. & II.

    D. I. & III.

    E. II. & IV.

2. Which of the following does not violate the statute?

    A. Proposition I

    B. Proposition II

    C. Both A & B

    D. Neither A nor B

If your exam includes overlapping options, divide them into individual options first. In our example, you would not look to the letters A, B, C, and D, but rather at each proposition: I., II., III., IV. Next, mark each one True or False, and then look for the right combination from the original options to determine the correct answer. This should prevent you from becoming confused and help eliminate wrong answers. Fifth, if you must guess, then eliminate as many wrong answers as you can and look for the most complete answer. Usually, but not always, an answer may be wrong because it is incomplete: perhaps only part of the rule is included, or the rule is stated incorrectly. If you must guess, choose an answer that is complete. Finally, never skip questions. If you come across a question that appears very difficult and you do not know the answer, don't save it for last; go ahead and guess, and move on. Do not waste time thinking about the question you skipped during the rest of the exam. You also don't want to make avoidable mistakes on your answer sheet, like misnumbering your responses.

Overall, most law school exams seek to evaluate the very skills that enable a lawyer to be successful in practice: (1) to listen to the client's "story" and separate relevant from irrelevant facts; (2) to identify the legal issue that is triggered by those facts; (3) to articulate the rules of law that govern that legal issue; and (4) to apply those rules to the client's fact situation and make a convincing argument to the court.

What to Do During an Essay Examination

Just as with multiple-choice questions, when taking essay exams you should develop a strategy and stick to it throughout the exam. Develop a strategy that you can use throughout finals. We suggest the following five-step strategy: (1) prioritize, (2) brain dump, (3) issue spot, (4) organize, and (5) write using IRAC.

Step 1 — Prioritize.

Before you read even one question, you need to determine how many questions you must answer, the point value of each question, and how much time you should spend on each one. Some professors will give you a suggested time limit for each question while others will list only point-value. Regardless, you must not spend all your time on the first question if it is not weighted the greatest. For example, on a three-hour exam with four questions of equal value, spend approximately forty-five minutes on each question. Do not sacrifice time allotted for other questions for finishing an answer to one. Keep track of time, and move on when time allotted for a particular question runs out; otherwise, your time for answering later questions will be insufficient. It is better to have a B on each question rather than an A on the first question, a B on the second question, a C on the third question, and a D on the fourth. By skimming the exam to determine point value and the time allotted for each question you can manage your time more effectively throughout the exam.

Step 2 — Brain dump.

The second thing you should do during an exam is something called the brain dump. It sounds nasty, but it ensures that you will not lose the vital information you've memorized in a panic situation. When the proctor tells you it's time to begin, turn to the inside cover of your blue book and "dump" out any key phrases, words, names, and terms that you associate with the course. Do not spend time organizing these items or putting them in any particular order at this point; just spew out all the information in abbreviated words and phrases. This process enables you to do two things: (1) it prevents you from panicking that all the information seeps out of your head, and (2) it places the terms in front of you BEFORE you read the exam, letting you see the terms and read with a purpose. Now that the necessary terms are down in black and white, you will consciously look for these issues when you read the questions, rather than read the questions and react to them automatically.

TIP: For the Brain Dump, use the "stream of consciousness" approach, and jot down **anything** on the subject that occurs to you. Possible terms in a Contracts course, for example, might include offer, acceptance, consideration, statute of frauds, unconscionability, parole evidence rule, counteroffer, and mistake.

Step 3 — Issue spot.

Having completed your brain dump, skim the entire exam quickly. Check to see which questions are assigned the most time and points, how many short answer questions (if any) there are, and the difficulty you may encounter on each question. As you go through each question, jot down the general area of law that the question appears to involve. On Torts, for example, ask yourself whether the question has more to do with intentional torts, or with negligence. Do not go beyond the big picture at this point. Remember, all you are trying to do is get a sense of the areas of law that are being tested and the point value of each question.

Next, decide which question to answer first. Unless your professor tells you otherwise, answer the questions in the order that you wish, as long as you label each question clearly. Sometimes, doing the easiest question first and building to the most difficult one makes most sense. This way, you build your confidence and feel prepared to attack

exam·essay ?

the more complicated questions knowing that you at least have conquered the smaller ones. Other times, it makes sense to start with the hardest, longest questions and end with the shortest ones. If your energy level wanes during an exam, start with the question that will require the most time and energy and then proceed to the easier ones. This process also ensures that you cover in the greatest depth the question given the greatest weight, thus minimizing the amount of points surrendered if you run out of time at the end of the exam.

Once you decide which question to attack first, reread that question very slowly, line by line. Each sentence should trigger something in your head: an issue, sub-issue, case, or defense. Perhaps the sentence triggers an intent issue for battery or assault. Jot down the issue next to each sentence. DO NOT JUDGE OR DISMISS ISSUES AT THIS POINT; just write them down. In other words, try not to simultaneously spot and disregard issues. If you spot the issue of consent, don't tell yourself: "Yeah, but it doesn't really work here." Just jot down consent. The time to judge will come. You may end up including or excluding the issue in your answer, but at this point, just jot it down. If you find that you have several sentences with nothing jotted down next to them, look back to your brain dump page, or to your flowchart or outline on an open-book exam. Do any of the facts in the question raise issues that match something in your brain dump sheet or flowchart? Try to match the facts to the issues. Although this process takes time, it is time well spent. It is much better to spend some time organizing your answer, rather than start writing only to have to go back and erase or change your answer. In order to help you understand this crucial step, look at the sample question below and a sample attempt at "issue spotting."

Sample Exam Question #3[2]—Contracts

National Bank agreed to lend Company $800,000 at 9% interest, provided that Company send a written response and a cashier's check of $16,000 as a "good faith" deposit within seven days. The president of Company did not respond to National Bank until eighteen days later, but nonetheless sent a response and a $16,000 cashier check. National Bank cashed the check. About one week later, the attorneys for National Bank and Company met and agreed on the payment method and fees. Two days later, however, Company was able to obtain a loan in the same amount from Local Bank at 8%. Company then requested a refund of its $16,000 from National Bank. National Bank refused. You represent Company. Can you get the $16,000 back?

Sample Exam Question #3 with "issue spotting"

National Bank agreed to lend *[offer]* Company $800,000 at 9% interest, provided that Company send a written response and a cashier's check of $16,000 as a "good faith" deposit within seven days. *[Specific form of acceptance required]* The president of Company did not respond to National Bank until eighteen days later, *[Did not "accept" as requested]* but nonetheless sent a response and a $16,000 cashier check. *[Acceptance or counter-offer?]* National Bank cashed the check. *[Acceptance of counter-offer?]* About one week later, the attorneys for National Bank and Company met and agreed on the payment method and fees. *[More argument for acceptance]* Two days later, however,

Company was able to obtain a loan from Local Bank at 8%. Company then requested a refund of its $16,000 from National Bank. National Bank refused. You represent Company. Can you get the $16,000 back?

Although some of the issues may seem obvious (National Bank agreed to lend [*offer*]), some are not so clear (Company nonetheless sent a response and $16,000 [*Acceptance or counter-offer?*]). At this point, though, your job is only to look at the facts and consider any possible issues or arguments, and jot them down. After linking most or all of the facts to some issue or argument, your next step is to organize your answer.

Step 4—Organize.

Now that you have marked possible issues to discuss, you need to organize your answer. Think of the question as a scramble. It is your job to unscramble it and make sense of it. Your answer will make more sense to the professor (and you) if you take the time to organize it. Several organizational methods can help, including making an issue-fact chart or outlining or flowcharting your answer.

One way to organize your response is to build an issue-fact chart.[3] List the issues and sub-issues you've spotted, and then jot down a word from the fact pattern that triggered this thought. Using the chart, decide which issues and sub-issues are primary ones and which are secondary. The primary ones deserve more attention in terms of analysis than the secondary ones, so make sure you divide your time accordingly. If, as you step back and look at your chart, overlap appears, you may need to eliminate something. Sometimes one fact sentence is applicable to two or more concepts. For example, one fact sentence may prove both acceptance and counter-offer. You can reuse a fact if you use it to prove something else. Very rarely should you eliminate an issue. Even if you think that it is not likely to succeed or you think it is weak, make sure you tell your professor why you discounted it. It might take only one sentence: "Although X may raise the issue of consideration given the words…, consideration is not likely to come into play because…." If you think an issue is not viable but don't explain it to your professor, your professor does not know whether you failed to think about it or just discounted it; therefore, make sure you explain your decision. See the sample issue fact chart for our contracts problem (*see next page*).

Issue	Sub-Issue	Facts
Offer	Intent	Agreed to lend
Acceptance	Specific form required	Written response and check within seven days
Acceptance	Did not accept as requested —mirror image rule	Responded 18 days later—11 days late
Counter-offer	Acceptance different— new offer	Responded 18 days later—11 days late
Acceptance of counter-offer		National cashed check
Acceptance of counter-offer		Attys met to agree on fees, etc.

If you outlined or flowcharted the course, you might try outlining or flowcharting your answer to an exam question. Note that this is a different type of outlining. Rather than provide general abstract information, you want to present the issue(s) and sub-issues raised and impose an order on them. One way to organize your answer is by party: who is suing whom for what? This is particularly helpful for Torts or Criminal Law, in which your exam could include many different people doing many different things. For example, if Joe, Jim, Ruth, and Anne are all doing tortious things to one another, you may consider beginning your outline like this:

I.   Joe v. Ruth

    A.   Battery

        1.   Intent—substantial certainty and unlawful

    B.   Assault

        1.   Immediate apprehension?

II.   Anne v. Ruth

    A.   Battery

        1.   Intent—accident

        2.   Harmful contact

Notice the cursory nature of this outline. You are not writing a complete outline; instead, you are simply organizing the issues you will discuss and the order in which you will discuss them. Do not spend a lot of time on this step. If you skip this step entirely, the exam answer will be disorganized and disjointed; if you spend too much time on this step, you risk running out of time in writing your answer. Make sure you allocate your time wisely. A rule of thumb is that of thirds: one-third to read, one-third to organize, and one-third to write. Obviously, this time division varies for different people. Whatever your division, make sure you spend the proper amount of time on each of these steps; otherwise, your answer will be difficult for your professor to read and to grade. Continuing with our Contracts problem, here is a sample outline answer to sample exam question number three.

I.   Company v. National

    A.   Offer

        1.   Intent—agreed to lend

    B.   Acceptance

        1.   Mirror image rule—not exactly same

II. National v. Company

    A.   Offer—same as above

    B.   Acceptance

        1.   Same as above

        2.   Counter offer—accepted—cashed check and atty mtg.

You can certainly flowchart your answer instead of outlining it. Again, remember that less is more at this stage of the game.

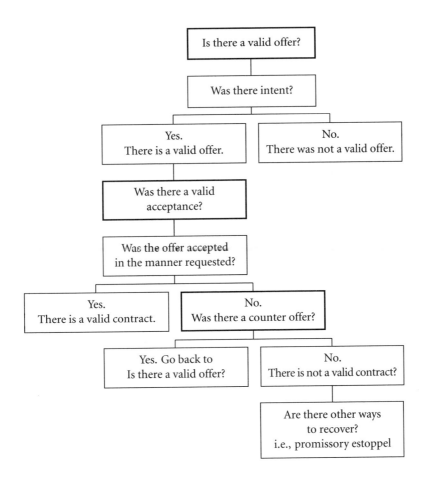

TIP: For addressing several issues, write about the one you know best first, and the one you know least last. Putting your best first creates a favorable impression as your professor reads your answer, and it builds your confidence as you move on.

Step 5—Write using IRAC.

Now that you've organized your answer, you can move on to IRAC. You may have several IRACs in any given answer, depending on the number of issues you found in the question. Sometimes, sub-issues are IRACable by themselves. For example, you might have a lot to say about intent, so much that it deserves its own IRAC. Just remember to focus on the sub-issues. Here's a sample answer to our Contracts question written in IRAC format.

Sample IRAC answer

Issue	The issue in this case is whether the communication between Company and National Bank constitute an effective offer and acceptance, or whether there was a rejection and a counter-offer.
Rule(s)	An offer is the manifestation by one party (the offeror) of a willingness to enter into a bargain with another (the offeree) on certain terms. For a valid offer, the manifestation must raise a reasonable expectation in the offeree that nothing more than acceptance is needed by the offeree to create a contract. An offer may be terminated (and no longer valid) if there is a rejection or counter-offer by another, or the time specified of the offer has lapsed.
	If an offer is made by one party to another when they are not together, the acceptance of it by that party must be manifested by some appropriate act. *White v. Corlies & Tift.* In other words, the acceptance must be communicated to the offeror.
Application Main Argument	Company will argue that National Bank's offer was no longer valid because the time for the offer to remain open had lapsed. Company will point out that the offer specifically asked for a written response in seven days, just as the offer in *International Filter* asked for a specific response. Company did not respond until eighteen days later, with the mailing of a $16,000 check, making its "response" a counter-offer. Company will also assert that National Bank did not accept the counter offer because National Bank did not manifest its intention to accept the counter-offer.
Opposing Argument	National Bank will argue that it accepted Company's counter-offer when it deposited the $16,000 check. National Bank will assert that retention of Company's check plus its silence constitutes an acceptance. Furthermore, National Bank will argue that Company was notified of National Bank's acceptance in the conversation between the attorneys for both parties in the meeting to discuss the loan fees and closing.

Conclusion   The court will agree with Company that (1) National Bank's offer was terminated, because the time for acceptance had expired, and (2) Company's counter-offer was not effectively accepted by National Bank because National Bank did not communicate its acceptance to Company; therefore, Company will be able to get a refund of its $16,000 deposit.

TIP: Five-step strategy for essay exams:

   (1) Prioritize your time,

   (2) Brain dump,

   (3) Issue spot,

   (4) Organize, and

   (5) Write using IRAC.

Exam Exercises

Exercise 9-1
Exam Question: Torts — Intentional Torts

Bonnie Richardson worked as a receptionist for First Federal Savings and Loan. One year, a Mr. Harry Henley began working at her branch. Mr. Henley worked in an office approximately thirty feet from Ms. Richardson's desk. Henley had been a pipe smoker for many years and had continued to smoke his pipe at work. Ms. Richardson hated the smoke. In fact, she had an allergic reaction to it that caused headaches and anxiety. Although she had a good attendance record at work before Mr. Henley's arrival, she began to get sick more often and missed quite a few days from work because of her headaches. Three months after Mr. Henley's arrival, Ms. Richardson was terminated, primarily for absenteeism. Mr. Henley was aware of Ms. Richardson's adverse reactions to his pipe smoke, but he was unwilling to stop smoking in the office, especially because First Federal was one of the few remaining employers not to follow the "smoke-free" office trend. Mr. Henley often taunted Ms. Richardson by blowing pipe smoke directly in her face and saying, "I'm your boss and you can't do a thing about my smoking; learn to deal with it or leave!"

Ms. Richardson has come to your law office for advice on whether she has a case for battery against Mr. Henley. Your partner has told you that she doesn't think intent is an issue, but she is concerned about the "harmful or offensive" aspect of battery. She wants to know whether Ms. Richardson will be able to satisfy this element of the tort.

Answer to Exercise 9-1

Issue/Fact Ladder

Parties	Issue/Sub-Issue	Facts
Ms. Richardson	1) Does Henley's conduct amount to harmful contact for purposes of battery? 2) Does Henley's conduct amount to offensive contact for purposes of battery?	1) Henley's smoke contacted Richardson both directly (he blew smoke in her face) and indirectly (his smoke reached her work area) 2) Henley blew smoke in Richardson's face while telling her she could do nothing about his smoking because he was her boss 3) Richardson suffered physical and dignitary harm and lost her job as a result of Henley's smoke
Mr. Henley	1) Does Henley's conduct amount to harmful contact for purposes of battery? 2) Does Henley's conduct amount to offensive contact for purposes of battery?	1) Office policy permitted smoking 2) Job termination was due to excessive absenteeism, not Henley's smoking 3) Contact was not offensive or rude because Henley merely stated the truth about the office smoking policy

Answer in IRAC

Issue
: The issue is whether Ms. Richardson, an employee, can satisfy the "harmful or offensive" element of the tort of battery, when the only "contact" is the blowing of smoke.

Rule
: The "harmful or offensive" element is satisfied when defendant touches, either directly or indirectly, anything connected with the plaintiff's person and when the plaintiff's personal dignity is harmed as a result of the contact.

Application Main Argument
: In this case, Ms. Richardson could argue that she has met the "harmful or offensive" requirement because Mr. Henley's smoke did contact her directly (he blew smoke in her face) and indirectly (the smoke from his office traveled to her reception area, some thirty feet away). She was harmed in that the smoke caused an allergic reaction, as well as headaches that allegedly led to the absenteeism that triggered her job termination; moreover, like the contact in *Fisher*, the contact in Ms. Richardson's case was also offensive. Mr. Fisher had a plate snatched from him in a public place while a restaurant employee yelled a racist remark at him. Similarly, Ms. Richardson had smoke blown in her

face, while her supervisor commented, "I'm your boss and you can't do a thing about my smoking; learn to deal with it or leave." Both comments, in a public restaurant and in a public office, would cause a person's personal dignity to be harmed because they are publicly humiliating.

Application
Opposing
Argument

Mr. Henley can argue that his conduct was not "harmful" because (1) the office policy permitted him to smoke, and (2) it is unclear from the facts whether his smoking caused Ms. Richardson's termination (i.e., she was terminated "primarily" for absenteeism). It is unclear whether she had other job problems and whether she was absent as a direct result of his smoking; however, because the standard is "harmful or offensive," Mr. Henley will lose unless he can show that his contact was not an indirect touching with plaintiff's person. Perhaps he can argue that smoke affecting someone who sits thirty feet away from him is a far cry from snatching a plate out of someone's hands; however, because he did direct his smoke at Richardson's face on occasion while making rude comments, it is likely his conduct is offensive.

Conclusion

It is likely that Mr. Henley engaged in harmful or offensive contact for purposes of the battery analysis.

Exercise 9-2
Advanced Exam Question: Contracts

Read and answer the exam question below using the strategy outlined in this chapter. First review Exercise 4-3, Synthesis: Contracts, from Chapter 4. Also note that, unlike the first exercise, in which you needed to argue only the facts, this question requires you to make additional arguments for both sides.

Joe Smith, a construction worker specializing in home remodeling, recently opened his own refrigerator sales and repair shop called "Joe's." Not knowing where to begin, Joe went to Carol's Refrigerator Supply to buy refrigerators. Joe and Carol had had previous dealings when Joe was in the remodeling business. Carol explained to Joe that his best option would be to purchase several refrigerators on an installment contract so that he would have to pay only a few dollars every month. Joe agreed with Carol's suggestion. Carol also explained to Joe that because he was getting a "special deal," the refrigerators would not come with any warranties or guarantees from the manufacturer. Joe did not quite understand what the warranty business was about, but agreed to Carol's terms without asking any questions.

Carol told Joe that he was getting a good deal and that he should sign up soon because others were "waiting in line" for refrigerators. Carol and Joe signed a contract that day. Although Joe saw the disclaimer of warranties in somewhat larger print, in the middle of a paragraph on page five (the contract was eight pages long), he nonetheless agreed to Carol's terms. Later that day, Joe reviewed the contract and calculated that he was paying 2% more than the market price for the refrigerators. Joe's wife, Rita, a law student, also told Joe that by excluding the manufacturer's warranties, Joe would be solely liable for any defects in the refrigerators. Joe wants to know if his contract with Carol is enforceable.

Answer to Exercise 9-2

Issue/Fact Ladder

Issue	Sub-Issue	Facts
Is contract valid?	Unconscionable/yes	Unsophisticated buyer — Joe is new to business
		Price is excessive — 2% over market
		Pressure to buy — others waiting in line, special deal
	Unconscionable/no	Sophisticated buyer — Joe has always been in business (remodeling)
		Joe has dealt with Carol before, knows her

Answer in IRAC

Issue	Whether Carol can enforce her contract with Joe in court will depend on whether the court finds the contract to be unconscionable. The determination whether the contract is unconscionable will, in turn, depend on the relationship between Joe and Carol.
Rule	If Joe and Carol were business people, a court would be reluctant to interfere with a negotiated contract. For example, in *Heller*, the court did not find a contract to be unconscionable when two sophisticated businesses were involved and the price for the product, according to the court, was not excessive. On the other hand, when the parties are of unequal bargaining strength, and when one party occupies a superior bargaining position, a different rule may apply. *Henson*.
Application Main Argument	Whether Joe is a sophisticated buyer is a matter of dispute. Carol could argue that he is in the business of refrigerator sales and repair and, thus, should know about prices. This argument is bolstered by the fact that we don't know whether the price in this case was excessive; did Joe pay $2.00 or $2,000 over the market price? Furthermore, Joe had been in the remodeling business prior to entering the refrigerator busi-

ness; accordingly, he would have had experience in dealing with materials and prices, and is not necessarily an unsophisticated buyer.

Opposing Argument

Joe could argue that he is in the business of refrigerator sales and was a victim of an unconscionable agreement based on the following: (1) Joe only recently opened his business; (2) Joe's former occupation was unrelated to appliances (i.e., he was a construction worker); (3) Joe purchased the refrigerators before he had a chance to review the contract; and (4) Joe did not notice that he was paying over market price until later that day (thus evidencing his lack of business sophistication). Fully understanding the terms of the contract is not the test for unconscionability (*Henson*), but the fact that Carol had ample experience in this business, and Joe had very little, plus the disparity in price for the refrigerators, may compel a court to find the contract to be unconscionable.

Even if the court enforces the contract, the question remains as to whether Carol's disclaimer (that Joe's good deal excluded warranties) is effective. Usually, for a disclaimer to be valid, it must be set apart from the text and obvious. *Bunge.* In *Bunge*, the disclaimer was in bold letters on the front of the contract. In this case, the disclaimer was buried in the contract (in the middle of page 5 of an eight-page contract). Joe could argue that in order to be effective, the disclaimer must be on the front of the contract. Carol can assert that the disclaimer was in large print and Joe, in fact, saw the disclaimer before he signed the contract.

Conclusion

The contract in this case is likely to be found unconscionable because of Joe's lack of experience in this business. If the court enforces the contract, the disclaimer probably is valid, given the large print and Joe's knowledge of the disclaimer.

Note that this exercise requires you to argue the facts and make arguments as to which rule the court should apply and how that rule will affect both parties.

Exercise 9-3
Exam Question: Civil Procedure — Personal Jurisdiction

Read and answer the exam question below using the strategy outlined in this chapter.

Ken is a Florida resident who collects baseball cards. He saw and responded to an ad in Professional Cards, a national magazine, for the sale of an excellent condition, original Babe Ruth rookie card. Dick, a Washington resident, offered the card. The next day, Dick mailed the card COD to Ken. A month after the sale, Ken noticed that the card had become discolored and blurred. Ken took the card to a professional appraiser, who determined that the card was a fake. Ken sued Dick in a Florida court. A Florida Long Arm statute provides that Florida courts have jurisdiction over defendants who "transact business" in Florida. Does the Florida court have personal jurisdiction over Dick?

Answer to Exercise 9-3

Issue/Fact Ladder

Parties	Issue/Sub-Issue	Facts
Ken	Can Ken sue Dick in a Florida court?	1) Ken is a Florida resident 2) Ken responded to an ad in a national magazine 3) Card that Ken bought through Dick's ad was a fake and not what it was advertised to be (and not as valuable) 4) Harm to Ken was inflicted by Dick from WA but suffered in FL
Dick	1) Is Dick subject to jurisdiction in FL courts? 2) Does the FL long-arm statute pertain to Dick's transaction, which occurred in FL? 3) Did Dick "transact business" in FL? 4) Did Dick purposely direct his contacts toward FL to enable him to meet the "minimum contacts" test of International Shoe?	1) Dick is a WA resident 2) Dick was not physically present in FL, nor did he consent to defend in FL 3) Dick placed an ad in an national magazine to attract customers from all over the country 4) Dick completed the sale by mailing the card to Ken in FL
Florida Courts	Does exercising jurisdiction over Dick in FL comply with traditional notions of fair play and substantial justice?	1) FL courts have an interest in protecting residents from fraud 2) FL courts have a duty to protect residents from harm by outsiders 3) The distance from WA to FL is great, but either Ken or Dick must bear the inconvenience

Answer in IRAC

Issue   Does the Florida court have personal jurisdiction over Dick?

Rule   Because Dick neither is present in, nor consented to defend in Florida, personal jurisdiction can only be established through a constitutional grant of personal jurisdiction from the Florida Long Arm Statute.

Application In this case, Florida's Long Arm Statute grants Florida courts personal jurisdiction over those who transact business in Florida.

Conclusion	Dick did transact business in Florida by advertising in Florida through the national magazine and by mailing the card to Ken in Florida.
Issue	The Long Arm Statute is not the only consideration. One must also consider whether Dick meets due process pursuant to *International Shoe*. In other words, the issue is whether Dick meets the "minimum contacts" test.
Rule	"Minimum contacts" are established when a defendant "reaches" into a particular jurisdiction for some purpose.
Application	In this case, Dick does because he purposefully directed contacts to Florida. He advertised in a national magazine, where a foreseeable probability existed that prospective buyers in Florida would read the magazine.
Conclusion	In fact, Dick sought buyers from anywhere in the country where the magazine was distributed.
Issue	Even if his contacts were isolated (i.e., only one instance of a sale in Florida is mentioned), will a court's exercising jurisdiction over Dick in Florida comport with traditional notions of fair play and substantial justice?
Rule	To decide whether Dick's contacts with Florida render personal jurisdiction in Florida fair, the court will balance all concerned interests.
Application	The court will consider Dick's inconvenience in defending a suit in Florida (a long way away from Washington) and Ken's interest in having the State in which he resides protect him, as a resident, from fraud. Also, the court will give great weight to Florida's duty of protecting its residents from harm by outsiders. Most likely, Dick's inconvenience of travelling from Washington to Florida will not carry much weight because he embarked to commit a fraud purposefully by selling a fake card.
Conclusion	Therefore, most likely, the personal jurisdiction grant by the Florida Long Arm Statute will be held constitutional, and Dick will have to defend the suit in Florida.

Exercise 9-4
Exam Question: Criminal Law—Actus Reus[4]

Billy Bruiser (who is a citizen of Statesville) recently suffered the loss of his pet Pit Bull, Killer. On that same day, Billy lost his job, and his pickup truck was stolen. Billy was extremely angry as a result of his bad day and went to his regular tavern to calm down. Upon arriving, Billy saw a stranger sitting on his usual bar stool. Billy proceeded to argue with the person and demand his chair. During the argument, Billy kicked the bottom of the stool, causing the bar patron to fall to the floor. Billy's day was complete when the police arrested him and charged him with battery. For purposes of this problem, assume that Statesville's statute reads:

Battery is defined as intentionally or knowingly without legal justification and by any means (1) causing bodily harm to an individual or (2) making physical contact of an insulting or provoking nature with an individual.

Has Billy committed a battery? Why or why not?

Answer to Exercise 9-4

Issue/Fact Ladder

Parties	Issue/Sub-Issue	Facts
State v. Billy Bruiser	1) Did Billy's act of kicking the stool out from under the patron fulfill the actus reus requirement for the crime of battery? 2) Did Billy's act fulfill the mens rea requirement for the crime of battery (i.e., did he both intentionally and knowingly act to bring about a result)?	1) Billy saw another patron sitting on his stool 2) In the course of an argument, Billy kicked the stool causing the patron to fall to the floor

Issue — Has Billy committed a battery? Has Billy's act of kicking the stool out from under the patron fulfilled the actus reus requirement for the crime of battery?

Rule — The actus reus for a criminal battery occurs when a person by any means (1) voluntarily acts to cause bodily harm to an individual, or (2) voluntarily makes physical contact of an insulting or provoking nature with an individual.

Application — Here, Billy voluntarily kicked the stool that the other patron was sitting on with enough force to knock it out from beneath the other patron; this constituted an act with intent to cause harm. Even though Billy did not directly touch the patron, his act was a physical contact with the person of the patron; the patron was sitting on the stool when Billy kicked it out from underneath him. Further, Billy's act was both insulting and provoking, which is sufficient to constitute a battery. Moreover, Billy knew with certainty that kicking out the stool from under a person would result in the person falling and possibly being injured, but Billy kicked the stool nonetheless.

Conclusion — Thus, Billy's act is sufficient to constitute the actus reus requirement for criminal battery.

Issue — Did Billy also have the requisite mens rea to fulfill the commission of a battery; that is, did he intentionally and knowingly commit the act constituting a battery?

Rule — Proof that an actor's mens rea is intentional occurs when the actor's conscious objective or purpose is to bring about a certain result.

Application	Here, Billy may not have intentionally kicked the stool with enough force to knock it from beneath the patron; however, the court may infer intent from the surrounding circumstances. For example, Billy's anger at the events of his day is clear evidence that he may have consciously wanted to kick the chair out from under the patron. Additionally, Billy's demeanor and act of yelling and demanding the chair is also evidence that he consciously wanted to kick the chair. Finally, Billy kicked the chair to remove the patron from the stool that he felt he should be sitting on.
Rule	Proof that an actor's mens rea is committed knowingly occurs when the actor is consciously aware that a result will occur with substantial certainty.
Application	Here, Billy or any reasonable person would be certain that by kicking the stool with enough force, it would move from beneath the patron. Billy's act of kicking was purposeful. The risk that the patron would fall was practically certain.
Conclusion	Thus, Billy intentionally and purposefully kicked the chair from beneath the patron, and his act satisfies the mens rea for battery.

Exercise 9-5
Exam Question: Criminal Law — Burglary

The state of Happy has the following common law definition of burglary:

> The breaking and entering of a dwelling of another at night with the intent to commit a felony once inside.

The law relating to this crime reflected a concern about a serious invasion of the right of habitation during hours of darkness, when the inhabitants are most vulnerable to attack and the invader most likely to escape recognition.

Mr. Green is a top executive with ABC Corporation, and Mr. Brown is his personal assistant. Although Mr. Green has a beautiful window office in ABC's downtown location, Mr. Green often works at home. His home office consists of a room, adjacent to his bedroom, with a desk, computer, and a file cabinet. Mr. Green has given Mr. Brown an extra key to his house and his security alarm code so that Mr. Brown can access his home office in case of an emergency.

In the past couple of weeks, Mr. Green has been upset with Mr. Brown's job performance. Mr. Brown has been preoccupied with an outside consulting project and, as a consequence, has been late with several assignments for Mr. Green. (No company policy prohibits outside consulting). Mr. Brown believed that he could catch up on his work for both ABC and his outside consulting if he had a laptop computer. Mr. Brown knew that Mr. Green had a laptop computer at home and considered asking to borrow it but decided against it because Mr. Green seemed upset all week. On Thursday of that week, Mr. Green informed Mr. Brown that he was going away for the weekend with his wife and children to get some rest and that he would not return until Monday morning. Mr. Green also informed Mr. Brown that he was displeased with his recent performance and expected a considerable improvement next week.

Upon hearing that information, Mr. Brown decided that he had to get the laptop right away. Mr. Green left for the weekend on Friday evening, and that evening at midnight Mr. Brown drove to Mr. Green's house. Mr. Brown used his key to enter the home and went directly to Mr. Green's office. Mr. Brown took the laptop computer, making sure not to disturb anything, and immediately left. Using the computer over the weekend, Mr. Green was able to finish his consulting project as well as his assignments from Mr. Green. When Mr. Green returned to work on Monday, he told Mr. Brown that his laptop was missing and that he was going to report it as stolen. Mr. Brown did not comment. Later that day, Ms. Goody (ABC's receptionist and the office gossip) noticed Mr. Brown with a laptop and remembered Mr. Green's missing laptop. She informed Mr. Green, who summoned security to search Mr. Brown's office during lunch. They found the laptop and arrested Mr. Brown for burglary later that day.

You represent Mr. Brown. At a hearing in this case, you moved to dismiss. At the hearing, the judge determined that the home office was, in fact, a dwelling, according to the common law. The prosecutor asked for a continuance, and the judge set the date for the next hearing to decide the motion to dismiss. Draft a letter to Mr. Brown detailing the arguments that you will make to prove that this was not a burglary, and whether you believe that you will win.

Answer to Exercise 9-5

Issue/Fact Ladder

Parties	Issue/Sub-Issue	Facts
Mr. Brown	1) Did Mr. Brown's act of entering Mr. Green's home at midnight and taking a laptop computer fulfill the actus reus requirement for the crime of burglary? 2) Did Mr. Brown break into Mr. Green's home at night? 3) Did Mr. Brown possess the requisite mens rea for the crime of burglary?	1) Brown is Green's personal assistant 2) Green gave key and access code to his office at home to Brown for emergency purposes 3) Green went out of town and told Brown to improve his performance before Green returned; after Green left, Brown used his key to enter Green's home and took the laptop computer 4) Brown used the laptop to complete work for both Green and others 5) Brown did not say anything when Green returned and told Brown that his laptop was missing

Answer In IRAC

Dear Mr. Brown:

You have been charged with burglary for entering Mr. Green's home at night and taking a laptop computer. Under Happy state law, a burglary occurs when (1) a person breaks and enters into the dwelling of another at night (2) with the intent to commit a felony. In your case, we face three issues. It is unlikely that the court will find you guilty of burglary.

Issue	The state must show that you entered Mr. Green's home at night.
Rule	The slightest entry into a dwelling place is sufficient to satisfy entry.
Application	Here, you entered Mr. Green's home at midnight, using the key and the security code he gave you to use in emergency situations. Although you were given access to Mr. Green's office, the office was accessible only through his home.
Conclusion	Thus, you unquestionably entered Mr. Green's home.
Issue	The state must also show that you broke into Mr. Green's home.
Rule	Breaking into a dwelling requires either actual or constructive force.
Application	You used the key and security code that Mr. Green gave you to unlock the door to his home. Thus, you did not use actual force to access Mr. Green's home. Further, Mr. Green voluntarily gave you the key and the security code to his home and gave you permission to enter in emergency situations. You did not gain access to Mr. Green's home by either fraud or threat of force. Thus, you did not employ constructive force to access Green's home because you were authorized to do so. Mr. Green may argue that you did not have authority to enter his home at the time you did, but I will respond that he authorized you to use your discretion in judging an emergency situation because he did not establish any more specific rules.
Conclusion	Thus, I believe the court will find that you did not use force to access Mr. Green's home and, therefore did not break into it.
Issue	Finally, the state must show that you possessed the mens rea, or mental state, to commit a felony.
Rule	The mens rea for the crime of burglary occurs when a person's conscious objective is to bring about a certain result, such as stealing a laptop.
Application	Here, you no doubt intended to take the laptop. You intended to use it to complete work for Mr. Green, a purpose he clearly authorized you to do. Further, when Mr. Green left, he demanded that you improve your performance. I will argue that in your judgement, you faced an emergency situation. Additionally, you were able to complete Mr. Green's assignments using the laptop. Mr. Green may claim that your silence when he advised you that he was reporting the laptop stolen demonstrates your

intent to keep the laptop. I will argue that you intended to return the laptop, but were afraid to admit that you had it at that moment for fear of your job; after all, Mr. Green had expressed displeasure with your performance just the week prior.

Conclusion   Thus, I do not believe the court will find that you possessed the mens rea for burglary.

Exercise 9-6
Exam Question: Torts — Policy Question

You are a trial judge in the state of Confusion. At trial, plaintiff introduces the following evidence:

Mama Stropus was walking her dog, Maya, in unincorporated Chaos township one morning. She has walked her dog several times along this particular route. The route takes her to a large open space in which she lets Maya run free. On this route one morning, she was crossing a neighbor's property (the neighbor had allowed Mama Stropus to walk over his property and often stops to chat with her), when two dogs, Killer and Brutus, pounced on Mama Stropus and Maya. Mama Stropus was knocked to the ground and sprained her ankle, and Maya, who got into a scuffle with Killer and Brutus, was badly hurt. The neighbor saw the scuffle but waited twenty minutes before calling for help. The neighbor does not own the dogs but has often seen them on his property and sometimes feeds them treats. When Mama Stropus finally got Maya to the vet, the vet opined, "If only you got here sooner, I could have saved her paw." Mama Stropus then went to her physician, who told her that the delay made her sprained ankle worse.

Mama Stropus' daughter, who went to law school, thinks that the neighbor is liable. Do you agree? Why or why not?

Answer to Exercise 9-6

Issue/Fact Ladder

Parties	Issue/Sub-Issue	Facts
Mama Stropus	1) Was Stropus a guest on neighbor's property? 2) Did Stropus contribute to her injury?	1) Stropus regularly walks dog across neighbor's property 2) Two dogs attacked Stropus on neighbor's property 3) Stropus and her dog suffered injury as a result of the two dogs attacking them 4) Stropus sought treatment for Maya before seeking treatment for herself

Parties	Issue/Sub-Issue	Facts
Neighbor	1) Did neighbor owe Stropus a duty? 2) Did neighbor breach a duty owed to Stropus? 3) Did neighbor's act or lack thereof proximately cause the injury to Stropus and her dog	1) Neighbor allowed Stropus to walk across property 2) Neighbor did not own dogs but has seen them on property and often fed them treats 3) Neighbor saw scuffle but did not call for help until twenty minutes later

Rule

A property owner is liable for harm when he breaches a duty of care to a guest and his guest suffers injury as an actual and a proximate result. Although a property owner owes no duty of care to a trespasser, he owes a duty to warn of known dangerous conditions to a licensee, and owes to an invitee the same duty plus a duty to make reasonable inspection to discover dangerous conditions and make them safe. Further, a property owner is strictly liable for injuries inflicted on a licensee or an invitee by wild animals or abnormally dangerous domestic animals kept on his land. A property owner has a duty to assist only when a special relationship between the owner and the injured plaintiff exists. A plaintiff is liable for any comparative or contributory negligence on her own part. A plaintiff also has a duty to mitigate personal injury damages by seeking appropriate medical treatment within a reasonable time.

Application

Here, the neighbor did not invite Mama Stropus onto his property, but he allowed her to cross it to reach the open space, where she let Maya run. The neighbor knew that Mama Stropus crossed his property because he often stopped and talked to her while she was walking across his lawn; therefore, Mama Stropus was a licensee, and the neighbor owed Mama Stropus a duty to warn her of known dangerous conditions on his property. However, he did not owe her a duty to make a reasonable inspection and make dangerous conditions safe because she was not an invitee. Although a property owner is liable for injuries inflicted by animals kept on his property, the neighbor did not own Killer and Brutus. Furthermore, he did not keep them on his property; rather, they came onto his property, and he gave them treats on occasion. Occasionally giving treats to two dogs that stray onto one's property does not amount to keeping them there.

Additionally, the neighbor could not have known that Killer and Brutus were abnormally dangerous because they never attacked him in all the times he saw them in his yard. Mama Stropus was not comparatively or contributorily negligent because she did nothing to provoke Killer and Brutus, and it is indisputable that Killer and Brutus's attack actually and proximately caused injury to Mama Stropus and Maya. Nonetheless, the neighbor was not strictly liable for Killer and Brutus and, thus, was not liable for the injuries to Mama Stropus. Even if the neighbor were liable for the injuries to Mama Stropus, her compensation would be limited. Mama Stropus had a duty to mitigate her damages by seeking appropriate medical care within a reasonable time; by waiting until Maya had been treated by a veterinarian and putting off her own treatment, Mama Stropus contributed to the worsened condition of her ankle.

Conclusion   Because the neighbor and Mama Stropus had no special relationship, such as that between a common carrier and a passenger or a parent and a child, Mama Stropus was a licensee permitted to cross the neighbor's property. The neighbor did not create a dangerous condition and did not put Mama Stropus into a position from which he would have a duty to remove her, therefore, the neighbor had no duty to assist Mama Stropus. Accordingly, as the judge in this case, I disagree with Mama Stropus' daughter and would hold that the neighbor was not liable for Mama Stropus' injuries.

Exercise 9-7
Exam Question: Constitutional Law—Due Process

Several branches of the armed forces, including the Navy, have promulgated regulations regarding the proper conduct of their officers. Specifically, there are anti-fraternization policies (senior officers are not permitted to have romantic relationships with junior officers), anti-adultery policies (officers who commit adultery can be punished), and policies forbidding officers from engaging in homosexual acts while in the service. Lieutenant Stephen Clark has been in the Navy for ten years. He is an expert in high-tech submarine weaponry. In fact, the Navy is one of the few establishments that has use for his high level of expertise. Although Clark wanted to pursue other areas of study, the Navy fostered and encouraged his particular expertise. He is super-specialized.

Clark married Ensign Mark Rodriguez, an officer junior to him, in Hawaii last June. Hawaii recognizes same-sex unions. The ceremony was held in secret, and only the two individuals and their immediate families attended. In addition to their personal relationship, the two have a professional association, as well. Clark is Rodriguez's commanding officer.

Despite their efforts to keep their personal relationship a secret (i.e., they mentioned their marriage to no one, and they refrained from public displays of affection), the Navy discovered the information through an anonymous tip and discharged Clark for violating the anti-fraternization policy and the policy banning homosexual activity. He has not been able to find employment since his discharge.

Clark seeks to challenge the Navy's regulations on due process grounds. What arguments could you make in his favor? What arguments do you anticipate the government making in reply?

Answer to Exercise 9-7

Issue/fact Ladder

Answer in IRAC

Issue	The issue is whether Clark was deprived of liberty when he was forbidden to (1) fraternize with whom he wanted, and (2) marry and engage in sexual expression with whom he desired.
Rule	The Due Process Clauses of the Fifth Amendment forbids the government from depriving an individual's life, liberty, or property without due process of law. Whether the government has denied an individual his liberty depends on whether the government has interfered with a fundamental right. Whether a right is fundamental depends, to a great extent, on the Court's interpretation. Some justices view only those rights enumerated in the Constitution to be fundamental (the textual approach), while others find rights to be fundamental if they are found within a collective, holistic reading of the Constitution (the penumbra approach).
Application Main Argument	Clark will argue that freedom to associate, marry, and express himself sexually are all fundamental liberties protected by the Due Process Clause. First, the right to associate is guaranteed in the First Amendment and is, therefore, fundamental because it is guaranteed by the Constitution. Second, under the penumbra approach, Clark will argue that the Navy, a governmental body, is forbidden from denying him such liberties. Clark will argue that privacy is a fundamental right in that the right to privacy can be inferred from a broad, holistic reading of the Constitution. The Court has found that this fundamental privacy right protects citizens from government interference with such things as marriage, procreation, and family. This case is no different from the others because it, too, involves interference with Clark's privacy to choose with whom he associates and whom he marries. In order for the Navy's regulation to be valid, it must pass the strict scrutiny test.

It will be difficult for the Navy to prove that it has a compelling interest in denying Clark his right to engage in homosexual activity or fraternize with Rodriguez and marry him, especially when none of these matters impacted his job performance. Further, Hawaii recognized the marriage and hence state law, which the government cannot arbitrarily ignore, is protecting the right. Further, Clark will argue that even if the Navy has somewhat of an interest in preventing fraternizing and homosexual activity within it, the policies completely banning both are neither substantially effective nor the least onerous means to meet those ends. Clark will assert that the Navy's end could be met in a less restrictive way, such as a policy against both activities while on the job and not "across the board." As it is, the policy is both over-inclusive (not all homosexuals are a job risk) and under-inclusive (many heterosexuals are a job risk).

Application
Opposing
Argument

The Navy will argue that its policies against fraternizing and homosexual activity do not interfere with a fundamental right and, therefore, do not violate due process. First, the Navy can argue that the rights to engage in homosexual activity and marry Rodriguez are not fundamental because neither can be found in the Constitution (the textual approach). Even if they were considered to fall within the "penumbra of privacy," the Court has limited its protections to areas concerning traditional family values. In other words, the Court has protected marriage, procreation, and family, but only within the bonds of a heterosexual relationship. Thus, the right to engage in a homosexual relationship would be distinguishable from other cases dealing with marriage, procreation, and family.

Finally, not only is the right not fundamental, it is also merely economic in nature. Here, Clark is being affected economically. Economic rights are not afforded the same protections as fundamental rights. The Navy will have to prove only that its regulation banning fraternization is rationally related to a legitimate government end. The Navy will argue that it has a valid interest in banning fraternization and homosexual activity. It will argue that it has a grave interest in preventing problems arising from emotional and sexual attachments within its unique structure, which mandates that members of the same sex remain together in close quarters for long periods of time. Further, the Navy will argue that fraternizing leads to favoritism, which is detrimental to order, even in private businesses. The Navy will argue that defending the country is, at the very least, a valid interest, which permits it to place these policies in effect.

Conclusion

The Supreme Court will probably find for the government. Although Clark has valid rebuttal arguments to the Navy's claims (Hawaii recognized his marriage and his case differs from previous ones involving homosexual unions), and this is more than interference with a mere economic right (the Navy lured Clark and contributed to his super-specialization), the current conservative Court will probably find in favor of the Navy. The Court has been reluctant to extend fundamental rights beyond those either enumerated in the Constitution or already held as such (e.g., contraception, abortion, sterilization, heterosexual marriage, living with relatives, child rearing, and education).

Endnotes

1. ©1993 Cathaleen A. Roach. Used with permission.

2. This problem and answer are based on *Houston Dairy, Inc. v. John Hancock Mutual Life Insurance Co.*, 643 F.2d 1185 (5th Cir. 1981).

3. Daniel Desario, Cynthia Lee, Alexander Shapiro, and Johnathan Tyler, (Brett Harris, Ed.), *Blond's Essay Series* (1992). Our issue fact charts are modeled from those found in *Blond's Essay Series*.

4. © 1993 Cathaleen A. Roach. Used with permission. Problem and answer based on *People v. Harrison*, 10 Ill. App. 3d 158, 294 N.E.2d 1031 (1st Dist. 1978).

Chapter 10

Time Management

Surviving in law school is an art, not a science. There is no "one way to succeed." Because law school has a strong competitive element, students are sometimes concerned that they are not doing enough or studying correctly based on what another student is doing. Do not let the anxiety of others rub off on you. Don't worry about other students. This is your money, your education, and your career. The best way to ensure success is for you to find what works best for you and then just do it.

What Works for You?

Referring back to our travel analogy, when you decide what trip you are going to take, you have to know yourself and what works for you. For example, do you want to cruise or fly? Do you prefer a warm climate or a cool one? Do you want to go out of the country or not? You must answer each question because each journey requires a different type of preparation. Analogously, you have to decide how, when, and where you study best in order to make the best use of your time while in law school.

How Do You Study?

College and law school differ greatly. In college, it was possible to pull an all nighter and perform successfully, especially when the exam required you to regurgitate memorized information. That approach will not work in law school, because law school requires you to engage in problem solving, rather than just memorization; therefore, overloading your mind with a million facts will not ensure your success in law school. Although law school requires thinking that is different from college, you can reflect on what study mode worked best in college when deciding how to study in law school. Are you a visual learner who learns best by looking at graphs and charts? Are you an independent thinker who prefers to work alone in a quiet environment, or do you prefer to work in study groups? Are you a kinetic learner who needs to practice to learn?[1]

When Do You Study Best?

Think back to college. Did you function better at night or in the morning? Do you find yourself up and about at 6:00 a.m. even on a Saturday? Does a boost of energy hit you in the afternoon at around 3:00 p.m.? Before setting up a tentative study schedule, it helps to know when you are most alert. Also know that most law schools will schedule classes for full-time day students throughout the day; therefore, you may have anywhere from an hour to three hours between classes. See the sample first year class schedule.

Sample First Year Class Schedule
Day Division Section A

Torts	M Th	9:00–10:15
	W	9:00–9:50
Civil Procedure	M Th	1:00–2:15
	W	1:00–1:50
Contracts I	T F	9:00–10:15
Constitutional Process	T F	2:30–3:45
Legal Writing I	W	2:00–3:15

Note from this schedule that the students start each day at 9:00 a.m., and most days classes do not end until after 3:00 p.m. Although they will spend over six hours at school each day, they are only in class for less than three hours! How they use the remaining time is up to them. Do you want to allot time for reading and reviewing before class or in between classes? Do you prefer to spend that time running errands and studying either early in the morning or in the evening? This is an important consideration when creating a study schedule.

Where Do You Study Best?

Do you have to treat law school like a job (*i.e.*, 9:00 a.m. to 6:00 p.m.) because of your other obligations? Do you require an environment of absolute silence that only a good library can provide? Do you prefer to study at home curled up on the sofa? Do you find it impossible to study without some background music? These are some things you should consider in determining where you want to do most of your studying. Some people find they cannot study at home. They may become consumed with "other things," such as cleaning or preparing dinner or everything under the sun (including organizing the sock drawer). All these things distract a student from studying. Some individuals are the complete opposite. They cannot take the silence of the library and must go home to study.

You should also consider whether you prefer to study immediately after class or whether you need some "down time" before diving into work. Do not feel pressured by other students who may immediately flock to the library after class. If you function best by allowing your brain to relax, then do so. Remember this is your education, and, to get the best return, you need to do what works for you.

Organizing Your Study Schedule

Once you decide what works for you, you need to organize your time. You should start by completing two different schedules: a semester schedule and a weekly schedule. The semester schedule will help you set aside blocks of time for working on larger projects, such as legal writing assignments, outlining, and practice exams. The weekly schedule will help you keep track of your day-to-day activities and daily reading assignments.

Semester Schedule

First, write down a list of what you need to accomplish. The focus here is on long-time goals and projects. This might include the dates of your finals and any mid-term exams, outlines for your courses, and due dates of legal writing papers and other written class assignments. Once you compile a list, you can mark due dates and goal dates for completing these assignments on a monthly calendar. Next, you should work backward, estimating how much time you need to spend on each project. For example, if you have a paper due in legal writing on the 15th, you might want to have a final draft done by 12th and the first draft done by the 8th. Knowing when you need to have the first draft done, you can make daily and weekly schedules to accomplish this goal. Use this same technique with exams. For example, if you have an exam on Tuesday, December 12, you might want to work backward from that date, planning how you will spend each day studying. The day before the exam, you may want to do nothing but practice exams. The day before that, you might spend memorizing the rules for that class. Before you memorize anything, you might want to finish your outlining and flowcharting. A sample semester schedule might look like the chart on page 136.

TIP: CAVEAT—This is merely a sample schedule. Depending on your own needs, you may need to schedule more time for memorizing and less time for outlining and/or flowcharting. Remember the key is to create a schedule to help you get organized, but recognize that you may have to modify the schedule as you go along.

To schedule time for outlining and flowcharting, you may need to think of your long-term goals. You might decide that mid-way through the semester, you need to begin working on your outlines. One option is to schedule several hours every weekend to work on your outlines. If you begin this schedule the first weekend in October and have four outlines to complete, you could have all of your outlines started by November. Then you can spend the remaining weekends finishing up your outlines, while you spend your study time during the week preparing for class. If you stick to this schedule, you can start doing practice exams during Thanksgiving break.

Sample Semester Schedule

Sunday	Monday	Tuesday	Wednesday	Thursday	Friday	Saturday
November			1	2	3	4
5	6	7	8 1st draft of Legal Writing	9	10	11
12 2nd draft of Legal Writing	13	14	15 **Legal Writing Due**	16	17	18 Torts Outline*
19 Contracts Outline*	20	21	22 **Thanksgiving Break Begins**	23	24	25 Civil Procedure Outline*
26 Con Law Outline*	27	28	29 **Last Day of Classes**	30 Complete Outlines		
December					1 Complete Outlines	2 Do Contracts & Torts Flowcharts
3 Memorize Rules for Torts	4 Do Torts Practice Exams	5 **Torts Final**	6 Memorize Rules for Contracts	7 Do Contracts Practice Exam	8 **Contracts Final**	9 Do Civ Pro and Con Law Flowcharts
10 Memorize Rules for Civ Pro	11 Do Civ Pro Practice Exams	12 **Civ Pro Final**	13 Memorize Rules for Con Law	14 Do Con Law Practice Exams	15 **Con Law Final**	16

* Assuming this student has been working on her outlines all semester, she set aside one full day at the end of the semester to add to those outlines.

Weekly Schedule

First, start by blocking off non-study time, such as commute time from home to school, meals (breakfast, lunch, and dinner), religious and/or family obligations. Then you want to make a list of your study goals for the week. Remember: you want to organize in a way that works for you. You may make a new list every day or every week, or you may put the list in your daily planner or calendar. Either way, by writing things down, you remember to do them. Once you complete a task, you can cross it off the list and take pride in your accomplishment. Also remember: you must prioritize your studying. For example, if you have Torts in the morning and Civil Procedure in the afternoon, read and brief for Torts before studying for Civil Procedure.

We suggest you begin by allotting three hours of study for each hour you spend in class. This includes reading for class, as well as reviewing your notes afterwards. Please note that because of the length, density, and language of some older cases, it may take longer to read and prepare for classes. (For more on reading in law school see Chapter 2.) With that in mind, make sure that you take advantage of every hour and manage your time effectively. This means not only devoting time to study, but also leaving time for yourself. Using the class schedule outlined earlier in this chapter, two typical study schedules of law students follow:

Study Schedule A

	Monday	Tuesday	Wednesday	Thursday	Friday
7:00 a.m.	Read Torts	Read Con Law	Read Legal Writing	Read Civ Pro	Read Con Law
8:00 a.m.	Brief Torts	Review Contracts	Review Torts	Review Torts	Review Contracts
9:00 a.m.	Torts	Contracts I	Torts	Torts	Contracts I
10:00 a.m.	Read Civ Pro	Read Con Law	Read Civ Pro	Read Civ Pro	Read Con Law
11:00 a.m.	Brief Civ Pro	Brief Con Law	Brief Civ Pro	Brief Civ Pro	Brief Con Law
12:00 p.m.	Lunch	Lunch	Lunch	Lunch	Lunch
1:00 p.m.	Civil Pro		Civil Pro	Civil Pro	
2:00 p.m.		Constitutional	Legal		Constitutional
3:00 p.m.		Process	Writing		Process
4:00 p.m.	Read Contracts	Read Torts	Read Torts	Read Contracts	Read Torts
5:00 p.m.	Dinner	Dinner	Dinner	Dinner	Dinner
6:00 p.m.	Brief Contracts	Brief Torts	Brief Torts	Brief Contracts	Brief Torts
7:00 p.m.	Relax	Relax	Relax	Relax	Relax
8:00 p.m.	Relax	Relax	Relax	Relax	Relax

As you can see from Study Schedule A, this person gets an early start to her day and is done studying by 7:00 p.m. She can spend the rest of her evening relaxing by herself or with friends or family. This particular schedule might work well for a typical "morning person" or someone who cannot study at home. This person can use the time in between classes and after classes to go to the library and study. You will also note that this schedule does not include weekends. This may be used for the student who wants to accomplish his or her reading and briefing during the week and use the weekends to accomplish larger projects, such as outlining and Legal Writing papers.

Study Schedule B

	Monday	Tuesday	Wednesday	Thursday	Friday
9:00 a.m.	Torts	Contracts I	Torts	Torts	Contracts I
10:00 a.m.					
11:00 a.m.	Review Civ Pro	Review Con Law	Review Con Law	Review Civ Pro	Review Con Law
12:00 p.m.	Lunch	Lunch	Lunch	Lunch	Lunch
1:00 p.m.	Civil Pro		Civil Pro	Civil Pro	
2:00 p.m.		Constitutional	Legal		Constitutional
3:00 p.m.	Read Contracts	Process	Writing	Read Contracts	Process
4:00 p.m.	Read Contracts	Read Torts	Read Torts	Read Contracts	Read Torts
5:00 p.m.	Brief Contracts	Brief Torts	Brief Torts	Brief Contracts	Brief Torts
6:00 p.m.	Relax	Relax	Relax	Relax	Relax
7:00 p.m.	Dinner	Dinner	Dinner	Dinner	Dinner
8:00 p.m.	Relax	Relax	Relax	Relax	Relax
9:00 p.m.	Read Con Law	Read Legal Writing	Read Civ Pro	Read Con Law	Read Civ Pro
10:00 p.m.	Read Con Law	Read Civ Pro	Read Civ Pro	Read Con Law	Read Civ Pro
11:00 p.m.	Brief Con Law	Brief Civ Pro	Brief Civ Pro	Brief Con Law	Brief Civ Pro

As you can see from Study Schedule B, this person, although also starting classes at 9:00 a.m., prefers to study later in the day, both after class and then later after dinner until 11:00 p.m. This particular schedule might work well for a typical "night person" or someone who prefers to study at home because this person can go home immediately after classes to study.

Whichever schedule you prefer, or even if you choose to mix the two, you need to make the most of every day.

Using Technology to Help with Scheduling

In doing what works best for you, you need to use all of your resources to make them work for you too. We suggest that you use technology to help you create and keep to a schedule.

If you are like most students, you probably have some form of a "smart" phone, like one using Microsoft Outlook, or a Blackberry, or an iPhone. If you do, consider using the calendar on your phone to include exam dates, paper deadlines, and set reminders. This can be helpful if you tend to procrastinate and/or get nervous if you realize you only have a couple of days left before a paper is due.

You might also want to consider using a spreadsheet program, such as Microsoft Excel, to plot out your weekly calendar. If you are very detailed and organized like us, you will find it really fun to see how much time it takes to shower or get dressed, and commute to school, and how you can find time to study when you think you are busy. Having the schedule in a computer program also allows you to modify it from week to week if you are working on long-term projects, such as papers or outlines. Caveat: Don't spend so much time editing your schedule that you don't get any studying done at all!

Finally, you can also use calendar programs that come with your email software. Email programs like Gmail and Yahoo offer free online calendars. You can share your calendar with your friends and some programs will send your reminders to your email address or your phone. This will allow you to stay on track with what you planned to accomplish. Whether you decide to get a good old-fashioned paper monthly calendar or state-of-the-art phone with all of the latest gadgets, explore the different calendar options and find a system that works for you.

Scheduling Tips for Part-Time Students

If you are a part-time student, either working during the day and taking classes at night, or taking care of a family or other needs and taking a lighter load of classes, you might find it more difficult to find time to study. We suggest you try to find time where you think you don't have it by trying the following. First, you can study on your commute to school or work (this is a great excuse to give the car a rest and take public transportation). You can use this time to read for class, review your notes from the previous week, or work on problems or practice exams. Alternatively, if you must drive, consider listening to tapes in the car. You can either tape your classes (get your Professors' permission first) or make your own review tapes when you finish each section. This will help you memorize the law and review what you have already learned. Second, you can set aside blocks of time to study in the evening after class or on the weekend. Remember: you want to be sure to set aside time for family and friends so that they don't feel neglected. Finally, consider using vacation time to complete larger projects, such as outlines, legal writing papers, and studying for finals. Taking a vacation day once or twice a semester may give you a much needed reprieve from work and other obligations to help you focus on your studies.

Setting Realistic Goals

Have you ever taken a trip somewhere and wanted to see everything; even though you knew it was impossible, you tried anyway. You think that if you are efficient, you'll be able to see every sight. You set a strict schedule, and when you are not able to see the fourth item on your list of twenty, you get frustrated and end up not seeing anything else. Creating a schedule for studying in law school can be quite similar. Often times, students set unrealistic goals, and when they cannot reach them, they become frustrated and adopt an attitude of defeat and decide that they cannot possibly succeed. To prevent this, think realistically. Realize that life sometimes gets in the way of our accomplishments. (For more on this, see Chapter 10.)

Although it will be important to stick to your schedule as much as possible, realize that you might need to change the schedule if something unexpected happens. If you find that it takes you longer to do the required reading for class, try to re-do your schedule and give yourself more time. If an old friend comes in from out of town and you find that you have lost an entire Saturday afternoon scheduled for studying, don't worry. Just realize that you have to make up for it on Sunday. Also, if you find that it will take you more than one weekend to complete your Constitutional Law outline, relax. Plan on working an extra hour or so every other night to finish it, and start working on the next one.

Finally, don't forget to schedule time for yourself. Although law school will be a full-time job (if you are a full-time student), you must make sure to take care of yourself. Make sure to exercise, eat right, and do a least one fun thing every week. Once you accomplish something, treat yourself. If you finish your Legal Writing paper a couple of hours earlier than you planned, go to a movie. If you set a schedule and stick to it for a week or more, go out and have dinner with your friends. This will help you appreciate the work you have put into law school and allow you to spend time with friends and family. Remember that a positive attitude may be the real key to success.

Endnote

1. For more information on different learning styles, see Lynn Murray Willeford, *What's your Style?* NEW AGE JOURNAL, September/October 1993 at 114.

Chapter 11

Additional Strategies for Success

Unforeseen trouble is a fact of life. Just as one doesn't plan on sickness or a lost wallet, one doesn't plan for personal calamity in the midst of law school. Nonetheless, it happens. Whether it is a minor inconvenience or a major dilemma, you have to deal with the situation, or the problem will escalate. Regaining one's balance after a minor inconvenience can be quite irksome, but a major catastrophe can be devastating; certainly we all have had trouble arise at one time or another that warranted taking a few hours, a few days, or even a few weeks from school or work. This chapter provides vital information for dealing with inconveniences in law school; consider it the concierge at the hotel during your travels, and refer to it when you need help with major problems or minor glitches.

What to Do When Life Gets in the Way of Law School

Law school does not stop when life gets in its way. Unfortunate things happen at the most inconvenient times: babysitters cancel, family members become ill, car accidents occur, thieves burglarize homes. Regardless of the problem, you need to devise a plan of action to resolve it. You are in a particularly difficult position if the resolution requires missing class or prevents you from finishing an assignment. Although not every problem lends itself to a quick fix, an immediate, thorough plan of action will serve you well in dealing with both the matter at hand and your assignments. The following action plan will get you through the trials of life in the midst of law school: (1) assess the situation, (2) contact school officials and review your options, (3) deal with the problem, and (4) get back to work.

First, assess the situation to define the problem and determine its severity. Is the problem sufficiently severe to demand months or years to solve? For example, are you coping with the death or serious illness of a close friend or family member? Has your spouse lost his or her job? Has your child care provider left town on a family emergency? You need to consider how long it will take to deal with the problem. A week or more, or just a couple of days?

After approximating how much time you will need to deal with the situation, go for help and examine your options. The Dean of Students or Student Affairs is the best starting point in determining your options. If this is a very serious problem and you need to drop a class or take an Incomplete, you must go through the proper channels to do so; see the Dean of Students to find out what those channels are. We cannot overemphasize the importance of informing school officials of your situation. Even if you think yours is a minor problem that you can put off and handle in a couple of days, it is better to be safe than sorry. Far too many students believe that they can tough it out and choose "just to get through" a situation rather than investigate other options, and too often, this approach yields unsuccessful results. Take finals, for example. Even in the most dire circumstance, it is impossible for the administration to undo a poor test grade. On the other hand, students who have informed the school of potential problems early are given greater consideration in times of need. By talking with school officials, you also determine which options are available. If you need to take a week off from school, administrators can inform your professors and sometimes obtain extensions on assignments. They can also refer you to services, counseling or otherwise, if necessary. Either way, it is best to know what's available should a need arise.

Next, you must take time to confront the situation. Law school requires 100% of your time. Many students find preparing for class the most time consuming aspect of law school; in fact, students often seek counseling for time management problems (See Chapter 9 on time management). Most law schools prohibit students from working during their first year because of the intense workload.[1] If outside matters suddenly demand your time, consider whether you have the time necessary to successfully continue with law school. When a major life crisis occurs, it's best to take a time-out from law school; a few days organizing and dealing with the problem, whether it is finding a new babysitter or visiting a loved one in the hospital, can save a lot of trouble down the road. Only you can decide whether you are willing to miss a couple of days of classes or more (after even a few days of law school, you will realize the importance of class discussion); however, taking a few days to focus on and deal with your situation may help you put your problem behind you, or at least get it under control, so that you can move on and get down to the business of law school.

Further, whether you decide you need to miss only a couple of classes or a couple of weeks of classes, be sure to explain your situation to school officials and family members. Certainly, everyone needs not know every little detail about all your problems, but when people know that you have a difficult situation on your hands, they can be supportive. It is easier to ask for help (in the form of taping classes and/or borrowing notes) when the reason is revealed. If you find yourself in trouble or need some help during law school, the following section will direct you to those who can provide the assistance you need to help you get to the final stage: back to work.

Where to Go for Help

Academic Support/Academic Assistance/Academic Achievement Office

This office provides services such as peer mentoring and classes and seminars on study skills, outlining, exam preparation, and time management. This office may be staffed by a full-time or an adjunct professor and/or student teaching assistants. In some schools, the Dean of Students may provide these services. This office is usually a fine resource for borrowing commercial study guides and practice manuals and for obtaining helpful tips on dealing with the rigors of law school.

Admissions Office

This office handles recruitment, selection, and admission of applicants for the law school. Some admissions officers are involved in other aspects of the law school from advising special committees to helping students with academic issues or handling financial aid.

Career Center

This office provides counseling for current students and alumni seeking employment. Often, the Career Center conducts workshops on resume writing, interviewing, and networking. Because many large law firms participate in on-campus interviewing programs, you may have an opportunity to find a job by interviewing on site. The most prestigious firms recruit only from the top 10–20% of the class and usually require recruits to be members of an academic honor society, such as the Law Review or Moot Court. By definition, only a small number of students reach the top ten percent of the class. Although the Career Center devotes considerable time to the on-campus interviewing program, this does not mean it neglects 90% of the student body. Indeed, many smaller employers, government agencies, and nontraditional firms use law school career centers to attract qualified employees. It makes sense to define and assess your employment goals and schedule an appointment with a career services counselor who can get you started on your job search.

Counseling Center

Some universities or colleges have a separate office for mental health services. These centers provide services to enhance students' skills and attitudes in adjusting to law school, ways to handle stress, and methods of relating to new people and experiences in law school. Of course, students are always welcome to visit the counseling center for personal problems outside of school. At the counseling center, students can meet and speak with trained psychologists, social workers, and/or staff psychiatrists who can discuss the problem or refer students to outside counselors if necessary.

Many law students are reluctant to use counseling services. Many believe that the isolation, dissatisfaction, and depression brought on by the pressures of law school will "blow over" on their own. Numerous articles have been written on the topic of law school stress and its devastating effects on one's sense of self (see Chapter 1 for more information). If you experience difficulty dealing with law school pressure, take the time to give the office an opportunity to help. The difference in a student's attitude is amazing when he discovers that he is not alone, and a good attitude may be the best defense against law school burnout.

Dean of Academic Services

This office provides a variety of services, from advising students on academic or personal problems to providing career services. This office sometimes provides services for students in need of academic support or special accommodations in their course work. In a small school, the Dean of Students, the Office of Disability Services, and/or the Career Center may provide these services.

Dean of Students/Student Services

This office addresses student quality of life issues. This is the office that students generally contact when an emergency arises, when they struggle with courses, when they need referral services, or when they seek information about law school organizations or departments. This office acts as a liaison between students and the rest of the school. Make a point of using it.

Disability Services

Many larger universities and colleges will have separate offices for students with disabilities. In smaller law schools, students will generally find that these services are handled through the Dean of Students or Student Affairs offices. To receive services, students must file an application through one of these offices and then a determination as to accommodations is made based upon the application and supporting documents. The goal of this office is to allow students with disabilities to become as self-sufficient as possible and provide services to enhance their learning and integration into the school.

If you've been diagnosed with a learning disability, make sure that your school's administration receives all necessary documentation and understands what you need in terms of accommodation. If you suspect that you have a learning disability, obtaining testing is in your best interest. Although it may be expensive, it's worth inquiring into the cost and procedure. Your success in law school should not be hindered by something that can be controlled, alleviated, or accommodated. By overcoming this obstacle, you may find success much more easily attainable.

Financial Aid Office

This office provides counselors who assist students who are in need of financial aid. They assist with scholarships, grants, and loans. In most instances, students will have to apply for financial aid through this office before school starts. In some schools, the admissions office also handles students' financial needs.

If, during the course of law school, you find yourself in need of an emergency loan, do not hesitate to contact the Financial Aid Office or the Dean of Students. Although they are not in the business of giving away handouts, and payment usually is not deferred until graduation, an emergency loan will help get you out of immediate trouble and let you get on with school.

Registrar

This office is charged with assisting students in registering for classes, withdrawing from classes, taking leaves of absences, and obtaining transcripts for official use. The registrar maintains official student records, and this is your first stop in updating your address and phone number.

Student Affairs

Generally, this office is closely connected to student organizations and student events at the law school. This office also handles counseling for students if not offered by the health services department. This office may also house the Dean of Students if he or she does not maintain a separate office.

Website

Virtually all law schools have websites that allow students easy access to information about services or directions on finding additional information about different offices in the law school, including e-mail addresses for faculty and staff. Some schools have tips for handling stress, time management, and exam preparation available online. Also, most websites provide links to other websites for valuable information about course materials, legal research, or law school in general. Plus, all this information is accessible from home, so you don't have to get dressed or wait in line for an answer.

What's the Problem?

Refer to the following for at-a-glance assistance in solving a few typical and not-so typical problems that occur both before and during law school.

Before Law School

I think I did poorly on my LSAT.

Law schools weigh LSAT scores *heavily*, mainly as a way of "weeding out" students that they do not believe will succeed in law school. You must look at your LSAT score relative to the other applicants. What is the mean and median LSAT of the school you have applied to? If, after looking at this data, you still feel that your LSAT is too low, then you have two options: (1) take the test again, or (2) live with your score. If you opt for the former, realize that different schools view multiple scores differently. First, all schools will see all of your scores. Some schools will average multiple scores, and others will evaluate your application based on the highest score. Therefore, most schools recommend you take the test only once. However, if you were ill, or ill-prepared when you took the LSAT, and believe you can do significantly better, you should consider re-taking the test. Keep in mind that admission committees consider college GPA, work experience, and the personal statement, among other factors, in evaluating candidates.[2] A significantly low score, however, may hinder your chances of admission, however great your "whole package" is. Look to the data provided in the application materials, and consult with an admissions counselor at the school(s) to which you intend to apply.

My college GPA and/or LSAT score are significantly lower than the median at my first choice school.

Although committees consider more than grades and LSAT scores, outside factors are unlikely to make up for substandard performance in college and on the LSAT. Be realistic; use a school's admissions profile as a gauge, not a discouragement. Again, consult with an admissions counselor at each school; they are in the best position to advise on the likelihood of admission. In most cases, they will be straightforward about your chances and will not fill you with false hope.

I was "wait listed" at my number one choice and accepted at my number two choice.

It's best not to accept admission to a school until you're positive about committing. Contact an admissions counselor at each school and let him or her know your situation; be honest with both about your intentions. Defer your acceptance decision as long as possible. If you find that your second choice school simply will not wait any longer and you still haven't heard from your first choice school, accept your second choice. Don't take a chance that you'll be accepted at your first choice school at the eleventh hour. You may lose deposit money, but you can withdraw from your second choice if your first choice comes through; if it doesn't, at least you're still going to law school, albeit elsewhere.

My financial aid doesn't cover all of my expenses.

If you find yourself in this precarious position, see a financial aid officer; he or she will know whether funds are available for additional loans and how to get them. You may have to work with what you've got; for instance, you may have to take a weekend job, or hunt down a roommate, or most likely take a personal loan. If you are resourceful, you may be able to secure a scholarship not available through school, such as one based on ethnic background. Depending on how short of cash you are, it may be best to postpone law school and work until you can afford at least your expenses while in school. Remember, interest piles up over three or four years, so borrow only what you need. It's best to pay off consumer debt prior to starting school; the last thing a law student needs is a credit card statement that won't shrink.

The bookstore doesn't have the books I need for class.

Although it should never be a problem, sometimes law texts sell out. Your best bet when this happens is to check out another law school; although different schools use different books, your chances of finding the Torts book you need is better at another law school than at Borders. You can also try an online service, such as Amazon.com (yes, it does carry many legal textbooks!) or LawBooks.com. Many areas have local bookstores that carry or even specialize in legal textbooks; these are logically (and conveniently) close to law schools. Another option is to check the library's reserve desk. Most professors will put both required and recommended books on reserve for student use in case of an emergency. Your last resort is to wait until another order comes in, which can take over a week; in the meantime, become friends with someone who has your book and offer to study with him/her.

I can't afford to buy all of the books I need for class.

The best way to avoid this pitfall is to prepare for the inevitable. If you're working through summer, set aside a hundred dollars per pay period for books; even used books are costly. If you still find yourself without cash at hand, see a financial aid officer; he or she can help you obtain an additional loan for expenses. If additional loans are unavailable, you may have to resort to credit. Your only other option is to buy used books from second or third year students; be wary of outdated editions.

During Law School

The First Few Weeks

I don't have any friends in law school.

Your law school classmates will be your colleagues one day. Colleagues will be in a position to refer clients to you, recommend you for a job, and offer networking opportunities. It is, therefore, crucial that you take a break from books and mingle with classmates. It is also important to build a sense of community and a support system. If you're shy and have a hard time meeting people, consider joining a student organization. Organizations provide companionship and moral support. Additionally, some organizations have national ties and may offer their own networking opportunities. Remember: it's your job to find employment after graduation, not the Career Center's. Start considering which law topics are interesting and meet people in those fields.

I want to form a study group.

The best starting point is the most obvious: look to your classmates. Ask someone you feel comfortable talking to whether he/she is interested in forming a study group. The Academic Support Office, the Dean of Students, or even the Student Affairs office may be able to refer you to other students or student groups interested in forming a study group. A caveat: although study groups can be valuable in the learning process by providing support, discipline, and feedback, they also can be destructive and counterproductive if not organized correctly. Three is a magic number; groups of more than three students tend to be less efficient and less thorough because individual members do not get the opportunity to talk out their thoughts. Also, study groups of more than three people lend themselves to developing cliques or alliances. Members should not only be friends, but should also balance each other's strengths and weaknesses. To ensure efficiency, study groups should agree on ground rules and set a predetermined agenda. The key to learning is the process of thinking and reasoning; the study group should never substitute for individual understanding (for example, delegating outlining certain courses to one member). The group should also constantly evaluate itself to determine efficiency and effectiveness; if it is not accomplishing goals, the best solution is probably to dissolve.

I'm a non-traditional student, and I'm experiencing a problem adjusting to law school.

> A non-traditional law student is any student who does not fill the mold of the typical full-time day division student coming straight from (or not long after) college. The non-traditional student can be a student from an ethnic or cultural minority group, an older student, or one who is choosing law as a second career. Some are married or work full-time and attend law school at night or part-time. Non-traditional students face difficulties unique to their non-traditional status. For example, juggling an existing career and/or raising a family while pursuing a law degree place next-to-impossible demands on students. Also, non-traditional students usually have been away from school for some time and find the adjustment more difficult than expected. As with traditional students, non-traditional students also feel isolated and alone because they often feel unable to relate to traditional students. If you are a non-traditional law student, develop a support group with other law students like you. Several opportunities are available. First, look to existing groups among your school's student organizations. You may enhance your law school experience through contacts made in organizations such as the Evening Student Bar Association, the Women's Law Caucus, or one of the ethnic student groups. However, if you find that no group meets your needs, consider starting one of your own with a few current friends. A suggestion: don't waste time complaining about law school and things that you cannot change (e.g., finals at the end of the year with no midterms); rather, use the group to discuss the pressures of law school, and share coping strategies. You can also use the group to review practice exams before finals. For more on practice exams see Chapter 8. You may also consider visiting the Academic Support Office for help getting back on track with the process of school, or see someone in the Counseling Center for help dealing with your frustrations.

Preparing for Class

It takes me a long time to read the assigned cases, or I'm having trouble getting through the required reading.

> The Academic Support/Assistance Office can help you sort through this dilemma. You have two possible issues. First, this may be an *environmental* issue. Make sure you read in an environment and at a time most conducive to learning. Focus on the material. If outside thoughts interrupt you during your reading, jot them down on paper and return to the task at hand; you can return to your thoughts *after* reading. (For more on choosing a study environment, see Chapter 9.) Second, this may be a *comprehension* issue. Reflect on what you aren't grasping, and try to figure out why. Are you reading cases using IRAC? (For more on reading cases, see Chapter 2.) Are you unfamiliar with the legal vocabulary? (See *Black's Law Dictionary* and write down any new words.) Are the concepts muddled? Although it may sound counterproductive, try reading something else before reading cases. Pick up a hornbook or commercial outline and review the topic **before** reading the case; again, the Academic Support/Assistance office can recommend a good source. This way, you have a basic understanding of the rules before turning to specific cases. Although it requires an extra step, this type of "contextual" reading eventually increases your speed, as well as your understanding.

I'm confused, while everyone else seems to be "getting it."

Isolation is a powerful feeling, but keep in mind that you are not alone. Law school will be very difficult at first. Much has been written about how isolating and psychologically taxing law school can be.[3] Realize that you are not the only one **not** "getting it." The students who seem to follow class discussion and are eager to participate are not necessarily grasping the material better than anyone else and are not necessarily the ones who will earn As. In fact, many quiet students do well on exams and many assertive students do poorly because they don't see the subtleties. Remember: exams do not test verbal skills. Practice exams will hone your writing ability.

I have no time for briefing cases; briefing seems to be a waste of time.

Briefing is the first step to understanding the process of "thinking like a lawyer." (See Chapter 2.) Briefing now will help you prepare outlines for your exams. (See Chapter 5). Also, remember that briefing will be hard at first, but with practice, you will begin to brief cases quickly. Use IRAC, which replicates the exam process; in briefing and on the exam, your task is to identify issues, recite rules, apply rules to facts, and conclude. By briefing cases for class, you are honing your exam skills. Seek assistance from the Academic Support/Assistance Office or the Dean of Students, either of which can help you in managing time and can recommend "contextual" reading aids. Remember: certain cases in different courses take longer to brief than others, so allot your time accordingly. You may spend three hours out of class for every hour of class time in Civil Procedure, while you may need only two hours for Torts. Set a regimen: spend one quarter of the time reviewing a hornbook or study aid for context or your notes from class to help connect the case to what you're about to read, one quarter of the time reading cases, and half the time briefing.

I find my professor especially overbearing in class. As a result, I am intimidated and silenced in the classroom, and am reluctant to contribute to class discussion. I do not learn well in this environment.

Scare tactics are not effective means of promoting student learning. Ask yourself whether the professor is unduly harsh with students, or whether he expects precise and well thought out answers; in other words, is the issue *attitude* or *approach*? If your professor is unduly harsh or demeaning, see the Dean of Students; she may let him know his students are not learning. However, if you find that he expects precision, which is more likely the case, consult the Academic Support office for tips on preparing better. Volunteer for questions you know the answers to. Listen carefully; some students find that the same answer that was wrong five minutes ago is suddenly right when tendered at a different point in the analysis. Ask the professor questions after class or during office hours. Although it is ultimately your responsibility to deal with the classroom, realize that the majority of learning will actually take place outside class. Classroom performance is not necessarily determinative of exam performance.

I'm not sure what constitutes plagiarism or collaboration in the law school context.

Most students realize that representing someone else's work as their own is plagiarism; however, students don't always recognize the many forms plagiarism takes. Familiarize yourself with this topic by consulting your student handbook, and ask your Legal Writing professor when in doubt. The rule of three words states that if you use more than three consecutive words verbatim, then you must attribute it to the source. Many cases of students' citing lengthy passages without proper attribution and improperly reading other students' drafts have harsh results; however innocent, these and many variations may violate the honor code. Make sure you know the particulars.

I am having a hard time with IRAC.

Your Legal Writing professor or Academic Support Office can help identify which part of IRAC you don't understand and explain it. Of all the parts of IRAC, students grapple with the application section most. The following are the most common problems and ways to correct them.

(1) *Problem*: The answer is conclusory without an analysis.

   Solution: Do not state who wins and leave it at that. You must explain *why* he/she wins. Correct this by using the word "because" as often as possible in your answer (think of the reader as a two-year old constantly asking "why?").

(2) *Problem*: No specific facts are included in the answer.

   Solution: Do not generalize; rather, use the specific facts given and apply the law to them. As you go through the fact pattern, check off the facts you use in the application. The reader should be able to reconstruct the problem from the facts in your answer.

(3) *Problem*: The facts and the law are isolated, rather than integrated.

   Solution: Structure your sentences using "This element is met or satisfied" and the word "because." Remember that you are matching law, or elements of law, to facts. You should not have a single sentence of pure law or pure fact; the two must be connected.

(4) *Problem*: The arguments are one-sided.

   Solution: Include the opposing view, then your rebuttal to that view (MOR— Main, Opposing and Rebuttal argument). See Chapter 2 and Chapter 8 for some examples of IRAC with MOR.

I bombed my first Legal Writing assignment.

See your professor immediately to determine what areas need improvement and how you can avoid those problems on future assignments. If you have problems with grammar or organization, find out if your school has a legal writing consultant or a writing center. If so, use this service for help on improving your writing. Don't forget that this is just one assignment and that you will have other chances to improve your grade; look at it as a learning experience.

I understand the cases and follow class discussions, but I don't enjoy law school. In fact, I despise going to class and find it hard to bring myself to do the work.

Many students develop a sense of not belonging sometime during their first year. For some, it coincides with a Legal Writing assignment, for others, with the large amount of reading and rigorous class discussions. Cope by venting to friends and family, or confide in a professor or your advisor. Take a weekend off after a hectic schedule and treat yourself like a human being. For some students, isolation is long-term and haunting. Ask yourself, "If I were guaranteed all As this semester, would I still want to leave?" If your answer is yes, seek out a teacher or administrator, or discuss your feelings with the Dean of Students or someone in the Counseling Center. You may have found that this career path is not for you.

Mid-Semester

I don't have time for the things I used to enjoy.

> This is perhaps the toughest aspect to deal with your first year, but as you progress, you will find that law school demands more time than you probably expected. Sacrifice is par for the course. Seek the services of the Counseling Center for advice on dealing with the feelings of being "trapped" in law school. Counseling can help you regain your perspective and prevent you from getting so caught up in school that you neglect your personal life. Take time out once in awhile, even just a day during the week, to see your friends and family, go outside, and exercise. Law school is demanding, and the Counseling Center can help you avoid letting it become a prison.

I need to start my outlines, but I don't know when or how to begin.

> About five weeks into the semester, you should begin creating an outline of all the material you have covered so far. You should look to Academic Support professionals, second and third year students, and the Internet for examples of student outlines. Remember that although other student outlines and commercial outlines can be helpful, creating your own outline is best. The purpose of the outline is to help you understand difficult concepts, sort through them, and arrange them into a logical, user-friendly format suited to your learning style. See Chapter 5 for some examples and more information on how to create an outline.

I want to drop a class or take an Incomplete.

> Contact your Dean of Students or your Advisor, the same as in undergrad. Either can advise you of your options, explain the repercussions, and address your concerns. Be aware of withdrawal deadlines at your school, as well as financial consequences.

I need to miss a week of school for a family emergency.

> Contact the Dean of Students, who can assist you in obtaining postponements on assignments if necessary. Also, be sure to contact your professors; letting them know that you will not be in class and obtaining your assignments demonstrates professionalism and shows you care about your studies. Finally, before you leave, make sure a fellow student you trust will be in class while you're not, and ask to borrow his or her notes. You may also ask him or her to tape record the class for you (make sure you get the professor's permission). If you are straightforward about why you won't be in class, you're more likely to receive a favorable response. If you don't know anyone well enough to ask, contact your professors, then see them upon your return about any questions you encountered on your own.

I am having personal problems that get in the way of academic achievement.

> See the Dean of Students, an Academic Support professional, or the Counseling Center immediately. Too many students think that they can shoulder

the burden of personal problems on their own while getting the semester "over with." Often, no matter how far out of your head you believe the problem is, it stays and surfaces at the most inopportune time. Schools do not change test times often, so resolve, or at least, confront the problem before finals. Schools consider options for a student who has encountered a truly traumatic event, but even the most legitimate circumstance appears suspect if it surfaces at the last minute. If you find yourself in a serious bind because you let the problem go until finals and it escalates, see an administrator as soon as possible. The Dean of Students may be able to have your exam postponed or some other accommodation made, but you must disclose your problem.

I'm having financial problems so severe I may be facing a desperate situation soon.

If your law school is affiliated with a main university, the university financial aid department may handle financial aid for all students. If your law school is "stand-alone," e.g., not affiliated with a university, financial aid is handled internally. In either case, the Dean of Students can help facilitate your aid, and in some instances, arrange for an emergency loan.

I thought I could attend law school and work, but now I find that I can't do both.

During the first year of school, full-time law students are prohibited from working more than 20 hours a week and are strongly encouraged not to work at all. If you must work to support yourself and/or pay for law school, you may have to modify your plan. See the Dean of Students or Academic Services to review your options. Many schools offer part-time day and/or evening programs that might better accommodate your needs. You may also explore cutting down on work hours and increasing financial aid; should you reach this conclusion, consult a financial aid officer. You may be better off extending the amount of time to complete law school, rather than trying to work and study and doing poorly at both.

Before Final Exams

I cannot take a final due to a family or personal emergency.

The Dean of Students may be able to postpone your exam or make some other accommodation based on your needs and your situation. Notify him or her *immediately.* He or she will direct you from there.

I don't know if I've assembled the information correctly or if my "big picture" is the right one.

Visit the Academic Support office. The process of putting all the parts of a course together into one "big picture" is the best way to prepare for the exam. Whether you put the course together by flowchart or by outline is irrelevant; what matters is that you put the course together yourself. The process mimics the one lawyers use in everyday practice. A good synthesis: (1) defines and describes topics and subtopics; (2) organizes material in a way that demonstrates how all the pieces fit together; and (3) illustrates the meanings of topics and subtopics with cases and hypotheticals. Focus on how well your outline/flowchart organizes information in a way that describes the process of problem-solving, not on whether the information is right or wrong.

My professor does not make practice exams available, so I have nothing to use for preparation.

> Many professors don't place practice exams on file for students. Some give mid-term exams, either for credit or for practice. If your professor makes any type of examination available, take advantage of the opportunity, even if you don't feel prepared. The purpose of the practice exam is to alleviate fear, as well as to review material. Students who take practice exams, regardless of their scores, do better overall on first semester finals than those who don't because they eliminate the fear factor. If your professor does not offer a mid-term exam, the Academic Support/Assistance office usually can help find a question in a study aid or another professor's file and may even be familiar with your professor's exam style. You can also look to the Internet for sample exams. Several schools, including Harvard, post old exams on their websites for student use. Ask your professor if she would be willing to take a look at your answer to a sample question. Most professors are happy to take the time, as long as they feel the student is making an effort to learn about the law school process, rather than just trying to get the answer.

During Final Exams

I am "blanking out" on the exam.

> If you have prepared by outlining using the process-oriented approach and by taking practice exams, then you should have confidence going into the exam that will act as a barrier to the "blank out" syndrome. Before you begin reading the exam, jot down key concepts and terms on a sheet of scratch paper or the inside cover of your bluebook to ensure that you will not forget key terms and that you will have them handy while reading the exam. If you find yourself panic-stricken, take a few deep breaths and tell yourself that you will write one sentence on the bluebook. Take a few more breaths and write another. If this doesn't work, see the proctor about taking a five-minute breather. If you find yourself in an impossible panic, ask the proctor to see the Dean on duty. You won't get out of taking the exam, but the Dean on duty may be able to calm you down and get you back on track and may even arrange for extra time afterward to make up for what you missed, depending on your school's exam policy.

I have a final and I'm sick.

> Contact the Dean of Students *immediately*. Although you no doubt will hear stories about previous students who took exams under extreme circumstances (such as labor), you certainly should not risk a bad grade by taking an exam when you're seriously ill. The Dean of Students can arrange for a postponement or other accommodation. **NOTE:** Your illness **must** be severe; you cannot postpone an exam because your throat is sore.

I've gone through the exam and discovered facts I cannot link to a legal issue, or I cannot spot a legal issue we spent much time on in class.

> Go through each question line by line, searching for as many issues as possible. If you discover facts you cannot link to a legal issue, go back to the list of phrases on the inside cover of the bluebook. Are any phrases unaccounted for? Do any

of the facts trigger these issues? If not, it may be a background fact. Do not obsess; move on, or you will sacrifice completing other questions. It is better to finish the remaining questions than to remain stuck on one fact. Although all professors do not test all issues covered in class, most include the majority of topics. Again, use your outline or flowchart or the inside cover of your bluebook to check your progress. Do you notice a disparity in your answers? For example, have you covered negligence in three separate answers but have yet to mention intentional torts, despite having spent three weeks on it in class? Quickly recheck your answers; could one of your negligence responses actually have been an intentional torts question?

I know I bombed the first final.

Sometimes you **believe** you have bombed a final, when in actuality you didn't (see Chapter 8). Going "back and forth" in your answer doesn't mean you bombed. If you made good arguments for both sides, then you probably have a good analysis. Wait for your grade before you panic, because you can't do anything about it once you've taken the final. If you turned in a blank bluebook, make an appointment with the Dean of Students immediately. Put the test out of your mind and move onto your next exam. Dwelling on how poorly you performed on one exam will not help you on the remaining exams.

After Final Exams

What should I do if I am in academic jeopardy?

You should immediately see the Dean of Students or Academic Services and the Academic Support or Academic Assistance person at your school. The Dean of Students can let you know your options, including the standards for probation and retention and what you must do to raise your GPA. The Academic Support professional at your school can help you improve your grades (*e.g.*, individual tutoring, counseling, or classes). For help on dealing with the emotional aspect of academic jeopardy and keeping your perspective, the Counseling Center is available. The worst thing to do in this situation is to take no action at all.

I finished my first year of study but have not gotten a paid summer/part-time legal job.

Not many first year students get paid legal jobs during their first summer. Most law firms hire second year students. First year students should contact the Career Center for opportunities in volunteer or intern/extern programs. Although you will not be paid, you will have a chance to network and prove yourself, possibly leading to a job later or even earning academic credit. You can also contact professors, who may need a summer research assistant. This way, you earn some money while developing your research and writing skills.

How can I get a job if I am not in the top ten percent of my class?

Although the top ten percent presumably has greater opportunity to find employment, the remaining ninety percent certainly are not out of the running. Many employers, especially smaller firms and companies, hire from the pool of graduates outside the top ten. Significant experience in a particular field as well as knowing more than one language certainly tips the scale in your favor. Like law schools, the majority of employers consider non-grade factors in evaluating potential employees; therefore you should look into writing on to Law Review, getting onto Moot Court, joining student organizations dealing with areas of law in which you hope to practice, and/or getting some practical experience while in law school through an intern or extern program or the law school clinic.

I have heard about Law Review and Moot Court but don't know what they are or how to get on. I don't even know if I qualify.

Law Review is a unique law school institution, and it is a prestigious honor to be a member. Law Review publishes scholarly articles written by professors and students. Each school has its own Law Review. Students run Law Review, which means the students decide what to publish. Students can get onto Law Review in one of two ways: "grade on" and "write on." Usually, Law Review automatically accepts the top ten percent or so of the class. Many Law Reviews hold writing competitions to allow other students to become members (hence the term, "write on"). It is in every student's best interest to participate in the contest; employers consider Law Review membership as evidence of exceptional ability. Members are required to research and write a scholarly article of their own. In the last year, members are eligible for editorial positions. Moot Court is another important organization that develops appellate advocacy skills. Although not as difficult to "get on" as Law Review, it is nonetheless another prestigious honor society to which a law student can belong. Moot Court members participate in various competitions that involve writing a persuasive brief and arguing the case before a group of judges. Moot Court holds competitions for new members. Contact the Student Affairs office for information on both of these organizations, or contact each office directly. Remember, too, that there are many other worthwhile student organizations besides Law Review and Moot Court, so don't limit yourself to the two "big ones."

By the time I graduate, I will have so much undergraduate and law school debt that I will need to land a big firm job in order to pay for my education.

As law school tuition continues to rise, debt becomes a more pressing concern. Realize that big firm jobs that pay big money are very difficult to get. In most cases, you must be in the top ten percent of your class just to get an interview. Big firms also consider Law Review and Moot Court experience, but this is not an option for everyone. A financial aid advisor can suggest ways to structure your debt given your realistic starting salary and help you determine the minimum to borrow. The financial aid office will also have information on other options, such as a loan forgiveness program for those who work in public interest law (if your school has such a program).

I want to challenge a grade.

Schools have their own policies, but generally, you cannot challenge a grade without an **extraordinary** circumstance, like bias or miscalculation. If you have a unique grievance, see the Dean of Students. Except for mathematical error, your grade will not be changed. Once you receive a grade in a course (which will be a month or longer after the exam), make an appointment to see the professor, especially if you earned a C or below. Ask to see your exam beforehand so you can be prepared with specific questions during your appointment. *Do not use the appointment time to argue your case.* The professor will not care whether you really know the material or whether others spent less time and effort; grades depend on one thing: the exam. Instead, use this as a learning opportunity to see where you went wrong. Did you miss issues, articulate incorrect rules, or fail to apply the rules to facts? Is your problem substantive (*e.g.,* you did not know the law), or is it process-oriented (your answer was not cohesive but conclusory or misinformed)? Learn from your mistakes and move on with your life (and law school).

I wasn't altogether truthful on my law school application.

Whether intentionally or not, you may have misreported or failed to report vital information on your law school application. **Do not overlook this matter.** See the Dean of Students immediately; although she must report all mistakes, omissions, or violations of the honor code to the Bar's character and fitness committee, she can help you address any mistakes as soon as possible. If you fail to correct the mistake, the Bar's character and fitness committee may exclude you from sitting for the exam.

I am experiencing racial or sexual harassment either from a professor or a peer.

Your law school should be sensitive to this situation, so you do not have to tolerate harassment. Refer to the school handbook or bulletin for the school's policy on harassment. The policy should spell out specific steps to take to resolve harassment issues. If the school does not have a policy, see the Dean of Students. If you are uncomfortable addressing the situation through formal channels, speak to an Academic Support Professional, counselor, or other trusted administrator or professor for advice. They may be able to address your concern without directly involving you.

Endnotes

1. The American Bar Association accreditation rules prohibit full-time first year law students from working more than 20 hours per week.

2. The Official Guide to US Law Schools, Law Services (1998).

3. *See* e.g., Lani Guinier, *Becoming Gentlemen: Women's Experiences At One Ivy League Law School,* 143 U. Pa. L. Rev. 1, 62 (1994). *See also generally,* Alan A. Stone, *Legal Education on the Couch,* 85 Harv. L. Rev. 392 (1971).

Chapter 12

Bridging the Gap as a 2L or 3L: What Else Can I Expect in Law School?

Life after First Year — What Should I Expect Next?

Life after your first year of law school should be similar to traveling after you have read all of the travel books and talked to the travel agent and booked your trip. Now it's time to board the plane or hop in the car and go! You will have a lot of options, ranging from taking classes and working over the summer, to getting involved in student organizations, local and national bar associations, as well as clinics, journals or other opportunities to gain real legal experience while in law school. So, you have to decide if you want to take the standard tour with a tour guide, or grab a map and make your way through the local neighborhoods on your own.

Every student in law school is faced with the choice about how involved they want to become in their individual schools. Some students simply do not have the time in their upper level years to spend on extra-curricular activities, as they have to work to pay their bills. Others have more time to spare or are specifically interested in one of the many programs that law school has to offer. Getting involved in school activities is a great way to get to know other students in your class while gaining exposure to the kind of law you would eventually like to practice.

Generally speaking, your "extra-curricular" options can be divided into two broad categories: academic and non-academic. There are things you can do outside of the traditional classroom to gain credit. Other activities will provide networking opportunities, as well as exposure to different aspects of the law. Some examples of the types of academic and non-academic opportunities for upper-level law students include:

Academic	Non-Academic
• Law Review • Journals, such as the Business Law Journal • Moot Court Society • Clinics • Externships or Field Placements • Guided Research	• Student Organizations, such as the Women's Law Caucus or the Black Law Student Association • National Bar Associations, such as the American Bar Association • Local Bar Associations, such as the DuPage County Bar Association, or the Hispanic Lawyers Association of Illinois

Law school itself is a micro version of the legal field. Each association or organization usually is geared towards a specific field or interest, and each member is usually looking for a career in such a field. Exploring the differences between each of the ways you can get involved is like exploring the differences in the various practices of law. It might take a few tries to find the perfect fit, but the information and knowledge you gain along the way contributes to your experience as an attorney. We will start by defining and explaining the academic opportunities and then move on to the non-academic opportunities.

Academic Opportunities

There are many ways to gain academic or course credit apart from sitting in a traditional classroom. These include working on a law review or journal, participating in the moot court society, working for a law school clinic and a host of others. We will explain each one separately to help you decide which one, if any, is right for you.

Law Reviews and Journals

Law Review is a unique law school institution, and it is a prestigious honor to be a member. Law Review publishes scholarly articles written by professors and students. Each school has its own Law Review. Students run Law Review, which means the students decide what to publish. Students can gain the honor of being "on Law Review" in one of two ways: "grade on" or "write on." Usually, Law Review automatically accepts the top ten percent of the class at the end of the first year of law school. Many Law Reviews also hold writing competitions to allow other students to become members (hence the term, "write on"). It is in every student's best interest to participate in the contest; employers consider Law Review membership as evidence of exceptional ability. Members are required to research and write a scholarly article of their own. In the last year, members are eligible for editorial positions and course credit, and sometimes tuition stipends.

Journals are similar to Law Review, in that they publish scholarly articles written by professors and students. Most schools have a variety of journals, each individually geared towards one specific type of the law. Journals also have write-on competitions which determine the various members and contributors. Similar to Law Review, journal membership is considered an honor and is valued by employers as evidence of strong writing ability. If you are interested in a specialized area of law, you should seek out schools with journals in that area, such as Business and Commercial Law or Health Law, so that you may have an opportunity to participate on the journal. Also, some journal members may participate as editors and receive course credit, and/or a tuition stipend. This varies from school to school.

Moot Court

Moot Court is another important academic opportunity. To become a member of the Moot Court Society, usually students will work in teams of two to draft a brief of 30 or more pages regarding a case, and then argue for one or both sides before a group a judges. The teams will advance until usually only two teams remain in the competition. Those two teams will argue for a final time and one will be declared the winner. The current members of the Moot Court Society will pick the winners of the competition, as well as others who drafted the "best brief" or made the "best argument" and invite them to join.

Moot Court members participate in various local, regional, and national competitions. Winning these competitions is not only good for the school's reputation, but can help quickly move an ambitious student along in a field of their interest. Each member will usually receive course credit as long as they compete in a competition. If you have any interest in becoming a trial attorney, or working in the public interest field, such as state's attorney's office or the public defender, then you should seriously consider competing for a spot on Moot Court. Some competitions for moot court can be geared toward a specific field as well, with some focusing on international law or criminal defense. Be sure you are applying to a moot court that interests you, both in the actual trial and the aspects of law discussed and learned through the trial or argument. The competition to make moot court at most schools can be very intense, and usually those who participate want to pursue that type of trial work as a full-time career.

Another aspect to consider for Law Review and the Journals, as well as Moot Court is the time commitment required. Usually the time needed to research and prepare a brief or scholarly article, as well as prepare for the Moot Court competition is equivalent to that of a part-time job or an additional course. Students on Moot Court and Law Review or a Journal are expected to attend regular meetings, check in with their editors or coaches, and, for Moot Court, practice their arguments often.

Clinics

A clinic is a law office within a law school that handles real cases, usually for low-income clients or not-for-profit organizations. Students may have an opportunity to work in the clinic, either volunteering or for course credit, under the direction of a law professor or an attorney who will supervise their work. Most law schools have a variety of clinics that are geared towards public interest, in a variety of fields, such as housing, criminal appeals, immigration or the death penalty. The clinics usually have a minimum required number of work hours per week, especially if the work in the clinic earns course credit. Clinics often require that a student, or a team of students, study and learn a case and take it on as their own. This real-life exposure to clients and how the system works in that particular field is what makes the clinic experience so invaluable. Plus, clinic experience is a huge resume booster.

The time commitment may make the clinic feel like a part-time job or an externship (see below); however, the experience a student can gain through such an experience is well worth the time. A student must know his or her own time restraints and be able to balance the hours the clinic requires and the rest of their school load, as well as any part-time jobs they may have. Having a passing interest in a field such as immigration will not be enough to keep you invested in the clinic; you must be prepared to learn as much as possible about a specific field.

Externship/Field Placement

An externship or a field placement allows a student to work for a government or not-for-profit agency, such as Legal Aid, under the supervision of an attorney and receive course credit. Because the student will receive credit, the student cannot also get paid for the work, and must have a certain level of knowledge, usually evidenced by completion of a set of required courses and/or number of hours completed. Most schools will also require the student to complete a certain number of field hours for the semester or term (usually 150–180 hours). The law school wants to ensure that the student is learning valuable legal skills and not simply making copies, so they will often require progress reports and supervision of an attorney for all work completed. An externship is a wonderful way to learn the ins and outs of the State's Attorney's Office, the Public Defender, or Legal Aid while also getting course credit. This is a great opportunity for a student to get a position to put on his or her resume and receive course credit. Finally, many students may receive recommendations for permanent positions after successful completion of an externship.

Guided Research/Independent Study

Guided Research and Independent Study allows a student to research for a professor and gain course credit. Usually with a guided research project the professor will pick the topic and the student may locate cases or law review articles and provide a synopsis of such, but may not do any significant writing. Usually with an independent study the student will pick the topic and research an area of law not currently being taught as a class and complete a scholarly paper or article as a final project. Both options allow the student to work under the direction of the professor and receive guidance and support, as well as credit. The number of credit hours is usually less for a guided research and the grade is typically pass or fail, whereas the independent study is sometimes for more credit and the student paper will be graded accordingly.

Non-Academic Opportunities

There are many opportunities to learn more about the law or volunteer to assist a particular cause or simply have fun. Law schools, like colleges have numerous student organizations, as well as local and national bar associations, which you may choose to join during your time in law school.

Student Organizations

There are many different student organizations in every law school. All law schools have some form of student government, such as a Student Bar Association, and many have organizations aimed at different constituencies and interest groups. For example, some groups are targeted towards a group of students, such as the Women's Law Caucus or the Black Law Student Association, and others are aimed at particular areas of law, such as the Public Interest Law Association or the American Constitution Society. There are even some legal fraternities, such as Phi Alpha Delta and Delta Theta Phi. A list of some law school student organizations follows. Please note that different schools will have different organizations.

Student Organizations

American Civil Liberties Union (ACLU)	International Law Society
American Constitution Society (ACS)	Intellectual Property Society
Amnesty International	Justinian Society
Asian-Pacific American Law Student Association (APALSA)	Latino/a Law Students Association (LLSA)
	LGBT Law Student Alliance
Black Law Student Association (BLSA)	Law and Science Society
Business Law Society	Moot Court
Criminal Law Association	Muslim Law Student Association
Decalogue	National Lawyers Guild
Delta Theta Phi	Phi Alpha Delta (PAD)
Environmental Law Society	Phi Delta Phi
Evening Law Student Society (ELSS)	Public Interest Law Association (PILA)
Federalist Society	St. Thomas Moore Society
Hellenic Law Society	Student Bar Association (SBA)
Society for Immigration and Asylum Law (SAIL)	Women's Bar Association

---

Each group exists to meet the needs of its members by providing mentoring, disseminating information of interest to the group, and hosting programs and bringing in guest speakers on various topics. Some of these student organizations have a national affiliate (such as the National Black Law Student Association (NBLSA)) and some members may have the opportunity to attend local, regional or national conferences for the group and serve on those higher levels.

All of these organizations offer opportunities for students to get to know other students outside of class, and opportunities to learn more about the legal field or a particular area of law. All students should at least attend the meetings or programs sponsored by student organizations, even if they are not members. More than likely your student fees will support the student organizations, so you are paying for these events and should take advantage of them. If you are interested in a leadership position in law school, you should look to the student organizations and decide which one is best for you.

Tips for Finding the Right Organization for You

- **Student Services.** If you need guidance about these organizations, seek out the Office of Student Affairs or the Dean of Students, who usually oversees them. Sometimes the Dean can give you a list of the student organizations available and answer your questions about the different organizations. Usually, during orientation or at the beginning of the year, there will be a fair or open house for all student organizations.
- **Talk to Other Students.** This may seem like the most basic of advice, but students are often intimidated by older classmates or afraid to branch out. Go directly to the student organization office(s) and talk to the students. Ask them any and all questions about what their organization does, and how you can be involved. Here you can find out if they sponsor several programs, bring in guest speakers or offer mentors to first year students. Usually the person in the office is an officer and will be excited about the organization and eager to answer your questions.

Local and National Bar Associations

Every major city or state has a bar association, and usually a young members section or committee that students can join. Simple online research will unearth such an association, which usually has a basic joining fee in addition to annual fees. Sometimes there is a very small fee or no fee at all for students. Once you are a member your level of involvement is up to you, but such an involvement can really help you meet practicing attorneys and other students who attend area law schools. Most bar associations will host annual cocktail parties or receptions, in addition to regular Continuing Legal Education (CLE) programs in which attorneys are updated on the current status of the law. Some events are free and there are fees for others, but the opportunity to meet practicing attorneys is invaluable. These events are designed for students and young lawyers to meet and network with other people in the field.

Whether you decide to "write-on" to a journal, participate in an externship, or serve as president of the Student Bar Association, you should seek opportunities to gain experience and network with your classmates while in law school.

Chapter 13

The Importance of
Gaining Legal Experience[1]

While law school professors stress the theory of the law and "thinking like a lawyer," employers value employees who have practical experience and can "do" things, like prepare motions, handle court hearings and execute discovery. The key, therefore, to landing a satisfying job after law school, is to gain some practical experience while in law school. This practical experience is similar to knowing enough about a city to conduct a tour for visitors. If you only read about the city, you might not be able to give the best tour and answer questions. However, if you visited multiple times (e.g. gained experience) you could take on the most curious of tourists. Your first opportunity to gain experience is the summer after your first year.

> Most law schools have a policy that first year full time students should not work. In fact, the American Bar Association has a rule that full-time law students cannot work more than 20 hours per week.

To find this first summer job, start early. Many legal employers begin recruiting for the summer as early as January. Of course, there are a variety of legal employers you might consider. Remember, the key is quality legal experience that builds your resume and evidences your ability to "do" legal tasks. We detail only a few of the many options you should consider.

Externships, Clerkships and Other Legal Work
Externships — Why, When and Where

Most law schools have programs that can help you find an externship. Visit your career office or externship office for more information. These positions are often with judges or in public interest, but can serve as great stepping stones into your legal career, and help you to decide what field you are interested in while earning school credit. Many externship positions are with government agencies that provide law students with great opportunities to research, write and attend depositions and court hearings. Keep in mind, however, that while the externship position may be invaluable for learning and honing your skills, they are not paid positions. However, in many cases, an externship only requires a minimum amount of hours in terms of commitment, so you can certainly take time in the summer to complete an externship while working.

Judicial Clerkships

Many judges, both in the federal and state court systems, rely on law clerks. Some hire full time attorneys as clerks, others hire law students. Those who do hire law students often look to 2Ls. The process can be very competitive. That being said, a judicial clerkship is invaluable. You will learn practical aspects about the system and see it at work on a daily basis. You will research and write memos relating to current events. And if you do a wonderful job, you may have a judge who can serve as a reference.

Research Assistant

Many professors hire research assistants to aid and assist them in their own academic pursuits. Professors can seek out such an assistant to help them in researching a project, editing a law review article, or working on a new class or research project. Again, the opportunity to research and write is valuable. Typically, assistants are hired for a semester, and have a minimum of required hours they must complete a week. Working closely with a professor teaches a student how to engage in in-depth legal analysis and critical discourse about an emerging issue or issues in the law. The professor can also serve as a valuable reference on a job application.

Internships/Summer Clerkships at Private/Public Entities

Most law students take on summer employment at a large firm, small firm, nonprofit or government entity. Unlike externships that provide credit, internships or clerkships of this vein are paid positions. The law school career center can help you find the list of all available positions. Start looking early. An intern basically shadows the attorney, learns how to interview clients, open files, research legal issues and prepare legal documents. The experience is designed to give you a first hand account of what it is like to work in that field or position on a day to day basis. Summer positions at large law firms are coveted not only for the salary that is available, but also because the summer posts often lead to permanent offers. On campus interviews that take place during the fall of your second year provide you with the opportunity to compete for these positions.

If you have worked as a paralegal or administrative assistant, you may have amazing practical experience and insights into the legal profession. However, most legal employers are looking for positions that give you a chance to act in the capacity of an attorney. Clearly, given the rising cost of law school, most of us have to offset the cost of education with a paying position. However, if you are working a job outside the legal field, make sure you find an externship or research opportunity that evidences to a future employer that you have begun your transition into a new career.

Writing a Good Cover Letter

Like all other types of documents, the writer must begin with the question—what is my purpose? What's the goal? A cover letter is the marketing tool that "sells" the information contained in your resume. It is not a transmittal letter—enclosed please find my resume; nor is it a regurgitation of the information contained in your resume. Instead, it is the document that tells the employer why you are the person for the job. Thus, it has to be persuasive.

The next question for any writer is, of course—who is my audience? For most large employers, whether governmental agencies, nonprofits or firms, there is a designated person who does the initial resume review. Usually, this person sifts through anywhere from 20 to 50 resumes per week. They can easily distinguish between a well crafted and tailored cover letter and resume and a generic "one size fits all" document. Luckily, the resume reviewer often tells you exactly what she or he wants to see in a cover letter— it's all in the job posting.

The best place to begin when crafting a cover letter is the job posting or description itself. Each employer has the perfect person in mind for the job when drafting the job description. Therefore, pay very close attention to the job description. It provides vital clues to what the employer is looking for in a future employee. Let's take the following portion of a job description as an example:

> The Litigation Bureau of the State Government Agency is seeking attorneys with sound judgment and excellent research and writing skills. A strong candidate will have a demonstrated interest in and enthusiasm for trial work and will also have 3 or more years of litigation experience, especially employment litigation experience and a demonstrated commitment to public service.

The words in the job description that have been highlighted provide vital clues for a candidate in terms of the structure of a cover letter. An astute candidate would devote a paragraph to each of the key attributes mentioned. In other words, the structure of the cover letter should be:

Excellent research and writing skills

Demonstrated interest and enthusiasm for trial work

Either employment litigation experience or demonstrated commitment to public service

The problem with most cover letters is that they parrot back these attributes in the cover letter without supporting evidence. Much like a poor exam answer, they are conclusory in nature. A good cover letter, by contrast, provides specific evidence; it builds a factual argument that supports the conclusion. Notice how the following cover letter starts off each paragraph with a very generic topic sentence, but then supports the assertion with specific examples and evidence. As we will see later, the resume is the document that lends credence to the assertions made in the cover letter.

Dear Ms. Smith:

I would like to be considered for the attorney position in the Litigation Bureau of State Government Agency. I have the research and writing skills, interest in trial work, and commitment to public service that you seek. In addition, it would be a privilege to work in State Agency.

Like all law students, I took the introductory class legal writing. Although I found the new structure and form to be challenging, I ultimately excelled in the class and chose to develop my skills by taking additional writing classes. In addition, I sought out research and writing opportunities. For example, I was a Research Assistant for Professor Carol Ramirez after my first year of law school. I conducted research on Prof. Ramirez's book regarding the influence of race and gender on promotion to partnership in large law firms. I was very enthusiastic about the work given its connection to my previous work with the Feminist League. In addition to the research, I edited several passages, maintained research files and detailed several footnotes. I also was a member of Western Law School's Arts and Media Journal. I was privileged when my article, "How the Internet Corrupts Copyright," was chosen to be published this past spring. I enjoy reading complex material, synthesizing it and using it to further a factual argument. My time at the journal also enabled me to hone my editorial abilities and learn the importance of attention to detail, such as citation and punctuation.

In addition to legal research and writing, I would also like to build my trial skills. While at Daly and Morgan, I was introduced to pre-trial practice. In addition to other matters, I worked on a medical malpractice case and conducted the research and drafted the motion to dismiss. I also assisted the senior associate in preparing for discovery by drafting interrogatories and document requests. Finally, I was able to sit in on several depositions in this case. All aspects of litigation fascinated me and I was fortunate to participate in the process. Although my litigation experience is limited, I now have a better understanding of how to draft motions and organize discovery. My experience at the Western Law School clinic also offered me an opportunity to interact with and advise clients. Therefore, I feel comfortable with participating in various aspects of litigation from client interviews to legal research and writing and can use these experiences to develop additional skills.

Finally, I have a strong commitment to public interest. I have participated in our law school's public interest society since first year. As a student lawyer in our housing clinic, I was able to put my commitment to public service into practice by assisting individuals with issues ranging from landlord/tenant disputes to mortgage fraud and looming foreclosure. I have had experience in the private sector as well, but I found that the opportunities that are available for new attorneys are more limited (due in large part to the billable hour requirement and client demands to minimize the number of attorneys assigned to a particular matter). I look forward to working for a government agency that is able to mentor a new hire. Moreover, the cases taken on by your Office impact the public sector in a way that is incredibly exciting. For example, the Smith v. Brown case has the potential of redefining wage discrimination in a way that will better people's, especially women's, everyday lives.

In sum, I admire the work and hope to contribute in some way to your mission.

Respectfully,

Jane Doe

GREETING

Let's turn to the greeting. You should never send a mass mailing entitled "to whom it may concern." Instead, do your research—find a particular name or at least use a professional title (Director of Recruiting) for your correspondence.

FIRST SENTENCE

Your first sentence should be precise and direct—I am responding to your posting for a summer law clerk position. Tell the recruiter specifically what position you seek. Do not indicate that you are open to any and all positions.

SECOND SENTENCE

Your second sentence should not be the standard "I believe I am the best candidate for this position." Quite frankly, at this point in your legal career, it is difficult to differentiate yourself from other candidates. Rather than start with an unsubstantiated statement, tell the employer why this particular position draws your interest.

IT'S NOT ABOUT YOU

Especially for newly licensed attorneys, it is important not only to emphasize why you are a good fit for the position, but why the position is a good fit for you. Many candidates will have the basic skill set sought; what sets one candidate apart from others is the genuine enthusiasm for the position. Therefore, do you research. If there is a particular case or issue that is emblematic of the organization's work, let them know.

SKILLS

Never overstate your abilities. No one expects a new graduate to have "extensive" trial experience. Even if you have had an opportunity to appear in court, do not equate that experience to trial work.

FAMILIAR WITH OFFICE OR LAW

Notice that the chosen case is a labor case. Although this candidate has no specific labor law experience, the reference to the case gives the reader a strong indication that she is familiar with the area of the law.

JANE DOE
1234 OAK STREET
CHICAGO, IL 60600
(312) 444-5555
JDOE5@AOL.COM

EDUCATION

Western University Law School, Chicago, IL
J.D. anticipated, May 2013
Arts and Media Journal Member and Articles Editor
Published: Comment, "How the Internet Corrupts Copyright", Spring 2013
Member, Public Interest Law Society

University of Illinois, Champaign, Illinois
B.A., Sociology, 2010
Member of Alpha Alpha Beta Sorority
Member of University Feminist League

EXPERIENCE

Western University Housing Clinic
Student Lawyer, Fall 2012
Assisted individuals with landlord/tenant disputes, housing matters, loan modifications and other legal matters. Counseled individuals regarding alternatives to foreclosure and met with representatives from mortgage companies to negotiate loan modification programs.

Daly and Morgan
Legal Intern, Summer 2012
Intern in a medium size medical malpractice firm. Conducted research in several cases. Research and drafted motion to dismiss in a malpractice case involving the liability of a hospital for a trainee anesthesiologist who ran out of oxygen before an operation was completed. Drafted interrogatories and document production request. Observed several witness depositions.

Western University Law School
Research Assistant, Summer 2011
Conducted research on the effect of race and gender on the promotion of associates to partnership in large law firms. Edited passages of the book, maintained research files and wrote several of the footnotes.

Notice how the cover letter corresponds to the resume. While the resume presents factual information—dates, numbers, experiences, the cover letter weaves all of this information into a narrative that explains how and why these past experiences make you a viable candidate for the current position. How do we achieve this level of persuasive impact? We tailor each cover letter and resume to each job description. In the age of computer cut and paste, it is easy to tailor these documents, yet too many applicants tend to universalize their applications. Taking the extra time and effort to perfectly tailor and fit your cover letter to the job you are applying for will make it stand out from the other applicants. If a cover letter sounds too generic, it creates the impression that this candidate doesn't necessarily want to work here, but rather is willing to work anywhere, in any field, just to get experience. While it might seem taxing to create different letters for each individual job description, the end result could possibly be you in a perfectly suited job! Remember, the recruiter is looking for THE candidate.

PHONE & EMAIL

Make sure that your cell phone has a professional greeting if that is the number you leave for a potential employer. In terms of email address, make sure it, too, is professional in tone. WILDjane is not appropriate.

GPA

With respect to adding in a GPA—as a recruiter of mostly lateral hires, I do not look for this number on a resume. However, many recruiters of entry level hires do, so if you are new to the job market, you should include this number.

DESCRIPTIONS

Be careful for how you describe legal matters. Client confidentiality is extremely important and you certainly do not want to disclose anything that is not in the public domain.

THE END

Notice that the resume ends here. Many are in favor of an "interest" section, but again, if the interest bears no relation to the job description, it is irrelevant.

Writing a Good Resume

Glance back at the sample resume. Notice that it is well organized, easy to read and provides the factual support for the cover letter. Like a good exam answer that weaves as many of the facts given in the hypothetical into a response, a good cover letter uses as many of the facts listed in the resume as a persuasive narrative of achievements. The purpose of the resume is to provide those supporting facts.

Most resume reviewers go to the resume first to get a sense of the facts. If the resume is organized in a way that makes it hard to understand, the reviewer usually stops there. If your resume is confusing and difficult to follow, how is it that your supervisor will be able to follow your other legal writing? Therefore, it is imperative to organize your resume in a logical, easy to follow manner. Notice how our sample moves from education to experience—a sound organizational method for someone new to the job market. Even if you have had extensive experience in a previous career, if you are new to the legal job market, education comes first.

Do not simply list the schools you attended and degrees you earned. List your achievements. Notice how the sample resume provides positions held in the journal and membership in clubs. Your activities in college, and your involvement in various organizations, are important to who you are as a student and a possible employee. Again, note relevance. In our cover letter, we described how and why these achievements bear upon our qualifications for the position.

When you write the experience section, do not limit yourself to paid positions. Make sure you list externships, clerkships, or any other practical legal experience. Remember, the section is entitled "experience", not "previous jobs." Notice that our candidate listed participation in legal clinic, a legal internship and research assistantship in her resume. In addition, there are succinct descriptions of the tasks performed. Be specific, without exaggerating your involvement, participation, and skills in the legal field. An employer wants to know the extent of your practical experience. It's not enough to say "conducted research." Instead, complete the thought—conducted research on what? What did you do with the research? Did you prepare a memorandum based on the research? Use it as a basis for a motion? Did someone else use it as a basis of a motion? No one expects a law student to have handled a case from start to finish, but we do assume that she has had some familiarity with the legal system. Inquiring minds want to know where you've been and what you've seen.

Finally, note that our resume is one page long. Although listing former employment without a description of tasks performed leaves the resume looking suspiciously bare, a resume that goes on for 2–3 pages is far too detailed. Remember the cover letter should be the descriptive narrative; the resume provides the underlying facts.

Tales from the Front or
One Recruiter's True Confessions

As a recruiter, I go through approximately 40–60 resumes and cover letters a week. On average, I spend less than two hours hour per week going through them. That's about 2 minutes per candidate. That's right—two minutes. So how can you impress me in two minutes?

First, follow directions. My website details application procedures. It specifies how your information is to be submitted, to whom and in what format. If you stray from the directions, I might get the impression that you might not be good at following your supervisor's instructions. Be conscious of proof-reading and spelling errors. The slightest incorrect spelling or formatting issue could cause your resume to be automatically discarded. Be mindful of the font as well. Larger than 12 point looks awkward, smaller than 10 point looks minute.

Second, do your research. Many internet job sites or career offices list opportunities that might have been filled. There might be other positions that are not listed. Rather than rely on second hand information, go to the source. Check the employer's own website when responding to a job posting. Commercial job hunting websites or even your own law school's career office might not have the most up to date information about a particular job opportunity. In addition, know as much about the employer's practice areas as possible. We have had several candidates applying to our estate planning bureau; sadly, we don't have one!

Third, do not disregard the job posting. I try to make my job postings as specific as possible. If the job posting specifically indicates that an applicant must be licensed in Illinois at the time of application, then I will not waiver from that requirement. Because 20 of the 40 or so resumes I receive weekly are from candidates who did not follow directions, my review is cursory.

Assuming that the candidate has not committed these three deadly sins, we move on to the review. I look at the resume first to get a feel for the facts. When did she graduate? From where? Accomplishments? Experience? I have my job description in mind when I do the initial resume review. Returning to the previous example, the job listing indicated that I'm looking for someone with research and writing skills, who likes trial work, public service and labor law. In the case of Jane's resume, I see some writing experience at the Arts and Media Journal, she participated in clinic and public interest law society (public interest is there) and she has had some pre-trial experience, but with medical malpractice, not labor. Based on the resume review alone, I decide to move on to the cover letter to see if she can convince me to go further. Yes, that's right. If your resume does not detail basic facts that I am looking for, I might not even read your cover letter.

If your resume indicates that the basic requirements have been met, I move on to your cover letter to see how and why you think your past experience translates into the current position. How and why does your experience demonstrate that you are good for this job? Quite frankly, if you cannot sell yourself in a cover letter, I doubt your ability to write persuasively in other contexts.

Other Tips

1) Despite advancements in technology, most law firms and legal agencies still prefer cover letters and resumes to come via regular mail, not email. Having a resume and cover letter printed on clean, thick resume paper with a matching typed envelope takes more time and effort than simply clicking send, but giving the prospective employer a hard copy of your information will leave a more substantial impression. Of course, make sure you check whether the potential employer prefers electronic or regular submissions.

2) Be as specific as possible about your experience. Hyperbole (extensive trial experience, superlative writing skills, ace researcher) does not impress the recruiter—facts do.

3) Beware ... of Facebook®, Twitter® and other social networking sites. More and more recruiters are Googling®, and searching Facebook® and Twitter® and other sites before extending an offer to a candidate. Please note that your reputation and character are at issue when you enter the legal profession. Does your page highlight excess drinking, sexual prowess, or other activity that might impress your friends but not your future employer? Think before you post or consider making your site private. There are privacy settings for all of these sites, which you can choose to control. Regardless of these settings, your friends might have incriminating or embarrassing photos of you. If you see something posted in regards to you, or that references you in a negative way, alert your friends or the site administrator to have it removed. You are now a professional, in a professional world. Drunken college memories do not need to be broadcast and shared for the world to see. Remember, once information is in the public domain it is PUBLIC to all.

4) Your past can also come back to haunt you — many government agencies also have authority (with your permission) to run criminal background checks. If you have any arrests in your past, it is good policy to disclose up front rather than wait until the employer discovers the matter through a background check. Many times, the type of arrest (misdemeanor v. felony), your age at the time (minor v. adult) and the disposition (charges dropped v. conviction) are weighed by the employer. Overall, your ability to disclose upfront and provide an explanation is also the better course — it demonstrates maturity and responsibility.

5) Never, ever, misrepresent your credentials — remember, saying so does not make it so. Stating that you have a certain experience in a field you know casually, or that you know how to write motions to dismiss when you've only researched the law for one, will lead the employer to expect that you can deliver on these claims.

The Interview

The resume and cover letter have gotten you this far, but the interview is your chance to shine. Keep in mind that the interviewers are evaluating whether you are the right fit for the position. Be prepared to elaborate on your cover letter — how do your past experiences translate into this new job? Why and how (be as specific as possible) do you fit the job description as posted?

Too many candidates sell themselves short. Compare the two exchanges (assume our candidate Jane has made it to the interview):

INTERVIEW #1

Interviewer: Jane, I see that you have no previous experience in the labor law field. How are you a good fit for this position?

Jane: Although I don't have any labor law experience, I am a quick learner and like to take on new challenges. I'm willing to work extra long hours to learn the law in this area.

INTERVIEW #2

Interviewer: Jane, I see that you have no previous experience in the labor law field. How are you a good fit for this position?

Jane: Although I have not worked on a labor law case, I have some trial experience in medical malpractice, which allowed me to develop a universal skill set (pretrial motion practice). Certainly, I still have to hone these litigation skills, but with a solid basis I can focus my attention on the subject matter. I have also studied labor law in law school and have followed your case of Smith v. Brown very closely, so labor law is not completely a new area for me. I am especially interested in Smith because of its potential impact on female workers. As a person who went to law school to pursue a career in public interest, I am a good fit precisely because of my passion for these types of issues.

Although the first answer isn't horrible, it's far too vague and clichéd. The second answer actually ties in past experience to current expectations. Notice that Jane never crosses the line and attests that she has labor law experience; instead, she ties in her previous litigation skills experience into litigation experience needed in the current position. Jane manages to mention her knowledge of trial experience without making claims beyond the actual experience. She also uses this question as an opportunity to highlight what she does know about labor law, the Office and the type of cases they handle, and her passion for public interest. As a result, the interviewer has the impression that she is a good fit for this position.

The newest research in interviewing techniques suggest that behavioral interviewing[2] is the best predictor of employee success in a new job. In other words, ask an employee how she has handled writing assignments, difficult co-workers or clients, tough deadlines and learning new skills in the past, and you have a good predictor of how she is going to deal with those things in the future. So, whenever possible explain how and why your past experiences make you an ideal candidate for this position.

It goes without saying that you must be at your most polished and articulate at the interview. Every detail counts, including: prompt arrival, professional appearance, manners, poise, and self-confidence.

Practice helps ensure that all of these qualities are met. Practice with anyone — friends, colleagues, family. Attend interview workshops to hone your technique (usually offered by your career office). And be prepared. Too many candidates treat an interview as an informal "just wondering what your office does" type of meeting. Even if the interview is a "courtesy" or "informational" one, treat it with the respect it deserves.

To triumph in the job search, students need to utilize the same skills that they brought to bear in their legal studies. They must identify the issues of importance to the employer by studying the job description carefully. They must articulate in their resume the underlying experience, with appropriate description that evidences experience. And, in the cover letter and interview, they must argue how and why the past experiences translate into qualification and enthusiasm for the new position.

Endnotes

1. Special thanks to Adelaida Otero, Recruiting Coordinator for the Illinois Attorney General's Office for her assistance with this chapter.

2. Unlike traditional interviewing, which focuses on the current position and skills, behavioral interviewing focuses on the applicant's reaction to past situations. For more information, see, http://www.quintcareers.com/behavioral_interviewing.html, http://www.quintcareers.com/sample_behavioral.html, http://www.uwec.edu/Career/online_library/behavioral_int.htm.

Last Words of Advice

We hope you found the material in this book helpful. You should return to some of the tips and exercises during your first year to review and reinforce your skills. During the journey through law school, you will hit some bumps in the road. However, we hope that this text will serve as a guidebook to keep you on track. Remember that if you prepare for the journey, remain open to the adventure and ask for help when you need it, you should bring back only good stories, new friends and overall success. Please feel free to email your travel postcards and stories to us at rstropus@atg.state.il.us or ctaylor@tourolaw.edu.

Dictionary of Common Legal Terms*

This short dictionary is an example of the most common and typically used legal terms. Here we present both their official legal dictionary definition, taken from Black's Law Dictionary, as well as the common meaning. We suggest that you invest in a good legal dictionary to reference as you read cases and run into new terminology.

Allegation

Dictionary Definition:

> The assertion, claim, declaration, or statement of a party to an action, made in a pleading, setting out what he expects to prove.

Common Meaning:

> An argument the plaintiff or party beginning the action intends to prove in her case.

Appellant

Dictionary Definition:

> The party who takes an appeal from one court or jurisdiction to another.

Common Meaning:

> The losing party in a lower court ruling who seeks to overturn the court's decision.

Appellee

Dictionary Definition:

> The party in a case against whom an appeal is taken; that is, the party who has an interest in upholding the original decision. In Supreme Court cases, the appellee is called the respondent.

Common Meaning:

> The "winning" party in a lower court decision who must defend the court's decision.

Certiorari

Dictionary Definition:

> Latin for "to be informed of." An order issued by a superior court to an inferior court requiring the latter to produce a certified record of a particular case tried in that court. The purpose is for the court issuing the writ to inspect the proceedings and determine whether there have been any irregularities.

Common Meaning:

> A Supreme Court grant to hear a case, usually because there is an unresolved or debatable issue.

---

* The "dictionary definitions" all come from *Black's Law Dictionary*.

Counterclaim

Dictionary Definition:

> A claim presented by a defendant in opposition to or reduction from the claim of the plaintiff.

Common Meaning:

> An argument presented by the defendant in opposition of the original claim by the plaintiff.

Defendant

Dictionary Definition:

> The person defending or denying; the party against whom relief or recovery is sought in an action or suit, or the accused in a criminal case.

Common Meaning:

> The party or person defending itself against an action or claim.

Indemnify

Dictionary Definition:

> To restore the victim of a loss, in whole or in part, by payment, repair, or replacement. To save harmless; to secure against loss or damage; to give security for the reimbursement of a person in case of an anticipated loss falling upon him. To make good; to compensate; to make reimbursement to one of a loss already incurred by him.

Common Meaning:

> To reimburse a party for a loss. Usually refers to a situation in which one party (e.g., an insurance company) has compensated a victim (e.g., the insured) for loss and now seeks to recover the money from the true wrongdoer (i.e., the one who caused the damage).

Injunction

Dictionary Definition:

> A court order prohibiting someone from doing some specified act or commanding someone to undo some wrong or injury; a prohibitive, equitable remedy issued or granted by a court at the suit of a party complainant, directed to a party defendant in the action, or a party made a defendant for that purpose, forbidding the latter from doing some act that he is in the continuance thereof, such act being unjust and inequitable, injurious to the plaintiff, and not such as can be adequately redressed by an action at law.

Common Meaning:

> A court order prohibiting a party from proceeding with a certain action, or requiring a party to take some action.

Jurisdiction

Dictionary Definition:

> The power of the court to decide a matter in controversy; it presupposes the existence of a duly constituted court with control over the subject matter and the parties.

Common Meaning:

The ability of a court to rule on the subject matter of the case and impose its judgment on the parties.

Plaintiff

Dictionary Definition:

A person bringing an action; the party who complains or sues in a civil action. A party seeking remedial relief for an injury to rights; it designates a complainant.

Common Meaning:

The party or person who begins or brings a claim or suit for another's wrongdoing.

Quid Pro Quo

Dictionary Definition:

What for what; something for something. Used in law for the giving of one valuable thing for another.

Common Meaning:

The giving of something by one party to receive something of value from another party; a trade or exchange usually called consideration.

Remand

Dictionary Definition:

To send back, as for further deliberation; to send back a matter to the tribunal (or body) from which it was appealed or moved.

Common Meaning:

A court decision to send a case back to a lower court to readdress a certain issue because of an error or misapplication of the law. In short, a "do-over."

Respondent

Dictionary Definition:

The party who answers a bill or other proceeding. In appellate practice, the party who contends against an appeal; the party against whom the appeal is taken, i.e., the Appellee.

Common Meaning:

The person responding to an appeal from a court ruling.

Summary Judgment

Dictionary Definition:

A procedural device available for prompt and expeditious disposition of a controversy without trial, when there is no dispute as to either material fact or inferences to be drawn from undisputed facts, or if only a question of law is involved.

Common Meaning:

A ruling deciding a claim in which the court finds no facts in dispute. In other words, all the facts favor one party.

Index